WOMEN IN THE WORKFORCE

WHAT EVERYONE NEEDS TO KNOW®

WOMEN IN THE WORKFORCE
WHAT EVERYONE NEEDS TO KNOW®

**LAURA M. ARGYS AND
SUSAN L. AVERETT**

OXFORD
UNIVERSITY PRESS

OXFORD
UNIVERSITY PRESS

Oxford University Press is a department of the University of Oxford. It furthers the University's objective of excellence in research, scholarship, and education by publishing worldwide. Oxford is a registered trade mark of Oxford University Press in the UK and certain other countries.

"What Everyone Needs to Know" is a registered trademark of Oxford University Press.

Published in the United States of America by Oxford University Press 198 Madison Avenue, New York, NY 10016, United States of America.

Library of Congress Cataloging-in-Publication Data
Names: Argys, Laura M., author. | Averett, Susan L., author.
Title: Women in the workforce : what everyone needs to know /
Laura M. Argys and Susan L. Averett.
Description: New York, NY : Oxford University Press, [2022] |
Series: What everyone needs to know |
Includes bibliographical references and index.
Identifiers: LCCN 2021049853 (print) | LCCN 2021049854 (ebook) |
ISBN 9780190093389 (paperback) | ISBN 9780190093396 (hardback) |
ISBN 9780190093419 (epub)
Subjects: LCSH: Women—Employment—History—21st century. |
Married women—Employment. | Women's rights. | Feminism.
Classification: LCC HD6053.A674 2022 (print) | LCC HD6053 (ebook) |
DDC 331.4—dc23/eng/20211117
LC record available at https://lccn.loc.gov/2021049853
LC ebook record available at https://lccn.loc.gov/2021049854

DOI: 10.1093/wentk/9780190093396.001.0001

1 3 5 7 9 8 6 4 2

Paperback printed by LSC Communications, United States of America
Hardback printed by Bridgeport National Bindery, Inc., United States of America

CONTENTS

3 How Do Women Balance Work and Family?   59

4 How Do Men and Women Interact in the Workplace?   95

8 How Do Women Fare in Retirement? 199

ACKNOWLEDGMENTS

The authors met in graduate school and owe sincere thanks to Dr. H. Elizabeth Peters, who served as their advisor and mentor and fostered their interest in women's economic lives. Since that time, the authors have collaborated on dozens of refereed journal articles and book chapters and co-edited (with Saul D. Hoffman) the *Oxford Handbook on Women and the Economy* (2018). The natural extension of that work was to make this area of research available to a more general audience. The present work represents the authors' combined sixty years of experience in the field and reflects the enjoyable and productive nature of their career-long collaboration.

This research is also informed by the authors' lived experiences as wives, mothers, and professional women, and they are grateful to their husbands, Richard Argys and Albert Folks, whose unwavering support made this project possible. Thanks are particularly due to Richard Argys, who painstakingly read and edited every word of this book, though the authors take full responsibility for any remaining errors. Exceptional research assistance was provided by Sumini Siyambalapitiya, Fan Guan, and Michael McHenry. The authors would like to thank their OUP team, James Cook and Macey Fairchild. Thanks are also due to the book's initial OUP editor, David Pervin, who encouraged the development of this work.

WOMEN IN THE WORKFORCE: AN OVERVIEW

Stories about women in the workforce permeate newspapers, magazines, and virtually all other media formats devoted to news and commentary in contemporary society. Women's movement into the paid workforce has transformed their lives—and the lives of their families—and has in many ways reshaped society. This book takes a holistic view of the economic lives of women in the workforce.

Adam Smith is largely viewed as the father of modern economics. The focus of his theories, as he explained in the *Wealth of Nations* in 1776, was on paid work in the formal labor market and worker productivity. Since women in that historical period devoted nearly all of their time to unpaid work (what we now term household or caring labor), it is perhaps not surprising that women were a nearly invisible part of economics. Their contributions to home and family were and often remain outside of standard measurements of economic activity.

Women's contributions are invisible no more. Two important changes propelled women into the mainstream of economics. First, when the United States entered World War II, women, particularly married women, surged into the workforce. As women changed their allocation of time from unpaid household work to paid work in the labor market, their labor began to contribute significantly to official measures of the country's economic production. As women continued to enter the paid workforce, they also began to make inroads as entrepreneurs and leaders.

Second, Figure I.1 illustrates many ways in which women's lives changed from 1960 to 2019. The figure shows that women began to marry later in life, have fewer children, and acquire more education—changes that are consistent with spending a far greater portion of their adult lives working for pay. During this period, women also made inroads into historically male-dominated jobs. Yet, because women usually remain the primary caregivers of children, issues such as work/life balance, equal pay, and the "glass ceiling" remain at the forefront of policy discussions in the United States and around the world.

In large part due to these changes, women's earnings as a percentage of men's increased from 60 percent in 1960 to just over 80 percent in 2019. Most of this change occurred in the 1970s and 1980s; the gender wage differential has not narrowed appreciably in the past twenty years. This book examines the importance of women's participation in the workforce, their contributions to the economy, and the challenges they face in claiming status, influence, and compensation equal to men's.

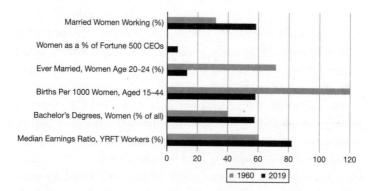

Figure I.1 The Transformation in Women's Lives from 1960 to 2019. Source: Adapted from Saul D. Hoffman and Susan L. Averett, 2021. *Women and the Economy: Family, Work, and Pay.* Red Globe Press.

Economists recognize that many outcomes that lead to gender disparities are the result of choices women make, but that they also reflect constraints faced by women based on social norms and laws. Nearly every chapter of this book considers how expectations of women as primary caretakers of their homes and families hinder their progress in the workplace. As women economists who faced some of these constraints ourselves, we view unfettered choice as a good thing for all women (and men). Hence, we argue that policies that remove barriers and expand opportunities are key components to achieving gender equality. It is important, particularly for policymakers, to understand when disparate outcomes in employment, occupation, and pay, for example, result from a restricted set of options.

This book focuses on what we know from recent and historical research, primarily by economists. What differentiates data analyses performed by economists from those in other social sciences is a focus on identifying and understanding causality. For example, economists want to discern whether advanced education *causes* women to work more, or whether a desire to work *causes* them to pursue advanced education. This is important so that effective policies can be designed. Economics research is constrained by the availability of data, most of which comes from surveys conducted over many decades. Although gender is a complex concept, many of these surveys allowed for only binary indicators of gender (male or female), and so these limited data necessarily inform much of what we know. When relevant data are available as part of economics research, we expand the view of gender beyond the binary. As survey methods and resulting data become more inclusive, the full spectrum of gender identities should be better represented in future research.

As economists and professors, we have nearly sixty years of combined experience and immersion in this literature. In this book, we give readers the benefit of our training by filtering through vast amounts of research and interpreting the evidence by highlighting and citing what we find to be particularly relevant. This work will inform readers of the complex choices, expectations, and constraints facing women in the workforce and the challenges policymakers face in addressing gender disparities.

1

ARE WOMEN AN IMPORTANT PART OF THE ECONOMY?

When people think about contributing to the economy, they often consider the work they and others perform in the job market. We start this chapter by explaining how women's involvement in the workforce has changed over time. We then ask how women's work compares to men's. For example, do women work as much as men? How much does women's work contribute to the economy? Are recessions different for men and women? To answer these questions, we have to think about how we define and measure work and the ways in which the specific jobs women do are different from those usually performed by men. Because most of the world's people live in developing countries, we also look at the patterns of work for women in these countries.

Spending is another important part of economic activity. You may have heard that, at least in the United States, women make the majority of family spending decisions. We take a closer look at that statement to see if it holds up under scrutiny. We end the chapter by noting that in many cases products designed for and marketed to women often come at a higher price than similar products designed for and marketed to men.

How has women's attachment to the labor force changed over time?

Women work. They have always worked. Historically, much of that work was done in the home and was therefore unpaid. This helps explain why men wanted wives. (Who wouldn't?) Nevertheless, women slowly joined the paid labor force, and their time and talents enhanced economic growth and were recognized with paychecks. To keep track of who is working, economists calculate the labor force participation rate (LFPR).

The Census Bureau measures the LFPR. Every month they conduct the Current Population Survey (CPS), a telephone survey of some 60,000 randomly selected households in which respondents are asked a variety of questions about the employment status of household members. These data are used to calculate the LFPR and the unemployment rate. This information is reported by the US Bureau of Labor Statistics (BLS) on the first Friday of every month.

The LFPR is measured as the percentage of the civilian non-institutionalized population (e.g., individuals not in prison, mental institutions, or old-age homes) aged sixteen or older who are working or actively seeking work. To be considered as part of the labor force, you have to be employed or be actively looking for employment. If you are not doing either of those things, you are considered out of the labor force. Figure 1.1 shows the LFPR for US women from 1948 to the present. For comparison, we also show the LFPR of men. As you might have guessed, men's LFPR is higher than women's, but the two rates have been converging over time.

Being out of the labor force can take many forms. You might be retired. Or you might be a student. Or you might be unable to work for any number of reasons (e.g., disability or the need to care for family members). Finally, as was the case for women—and still is for many people, including increasing numbers of men—you might be working at home without compensation from an employer. In fact, as recently as the 1970

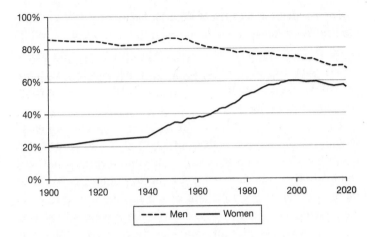

Figure 1.1 Labor Force Participation Rates of US Men and Women, 1900–2020
Source: BLS.

Census, the government had a category titled "keeping house" when collecting data on work activities.

Digging into some Census archives provides a glimpse of women's LFPR even before the 1940s. Around 1890, for example, women's labor force participation was quite low. Generally, the only women who worked for pay were either single, non-white, immigrants, or women whose husbands did not earn enough to support them. For example, single women had a LFPR of 46 percent, but married women had an LFPR of 6 percent—quite a difference![1]

Moving forward, the 1940 Census reports the LFPR of single women as 45 percent, compared to that of married women at 14.7 percent—still quite different, but the gap had begun to narrow. Until the early 1940s, there were "marriage bars"—a set of laws and employer policies that prohibited the hiring of married women, particularly as teachers and in some clerical jobs. These bars were partly responsible for explaining the low LFPR of married women in this time period but were largely gone by the 1950s.

The participation of the United States in World War II ushered in a new perspective on women in the workplace. While some women worked during the war and then returned to "keeping house" afterward, others remained in the labor force. Certainly, World War II helped normalize the idea of women working outside the home.

The trend continued, and by 1970 over 42 percent of all women in the United States participated in the labor force. Doubtless, the introduction of oral contraceptives and the legalization of abortion allowed more women to work, as these afforded women control of the timing and spacing of their births. As shown in Figure 1.2, there were still sizable differences across marital status, with 53 percent of single women working versus approximately 40 percent of married women. Over a thirty-year period, that is remarkably rapid change.

There are pronounced differences between the LFPRs of Black and white women over time. Historically, and largely due to the abhorrent, 400-year practice of slavery and subsequent racial discrimination in the United States, Black women have almost always worked at higher rates than white women,

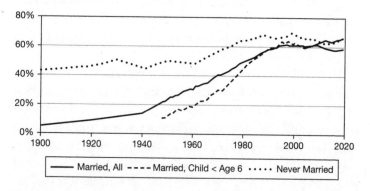

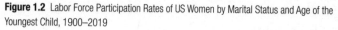

Figure 1.2 Labor Force Participation Rates of US Women by Marital Status and Age of the Youngest Child, 1900–2019

Source: BLS.

although the gap has narrowed substantially in the last four decades or so, as shown in Figure 1.3.

A study tracked down the origins of this Black/white difference in LFPR and linked it to the history of slavery in the United States.[2] Specifically, the researchers found that women who were the daughters of enslaved people were more likely to work, and they examined possible reasons for this. First, the daughters of enslaved people saw their mothers working and viewed work outside the home as expected and not unusual. Second, their mothers were more likely to work in low-skilled jobs. Consequently, many of these jobs, deemed too dirty or dangerous for white women, were seen as socially acceptable for Black women. Another factor contributing to the higher LFPR of Black women is the lower earnings of their husbands—also a legacy of the history of racial discrimination in the United States.[3] This makes it more likely that married

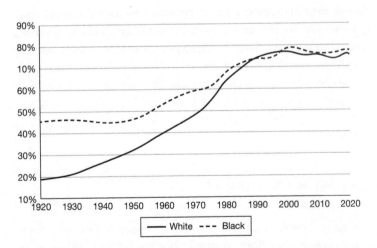

Figure 1.3 Labor Force Participation Rates of US Women Aged 25–54 by Race, 1920–2020

Source: 1920–1970 adapted from Boustan, Leah Platt and William J. Collins. "The origin and persistence of black-white differences in women's labor force participation." in *Human Capital in History: The American Record*. Chicago: University of Chicago Press. (2014): 205–240, Appendix Table A1. 1975–2020, BLS.

Black couples need two incomes compared to their white counterparts.

Another dimension of differences in LFPR is related to education. In the early part of the twentieth century, women with less education were often those who worked, and they primarily worked in manufacturing or as housekeepers or laundresses. Because these jobs required little education and offered few opportunities for advancement—these certainly were not careers as we use that word today—it did not pay for women to invest in their schooling. With a lack of career opportunities, well-educated women were largely absent from the workforce. Of course, even during this period, some educated women did work as teachers, but it was the advent of technological change, which ushered in administrative jobs that were deemed suitable for more educated women, that enabled these women to enter the workforce in larger numbers.

In her presidential address to the American Economic Association, Claudia Goldin, an economist who has spent her career exploring dusty archives of historical data so that the rest of us can understand the economic lives of women, asserted that "women's increased involvement in the economy was the most significant change in labor markets during the past century."[4] And significant it is. One estimate indicates that if women had not increased their work hours after 1979, the output of the US economy in 2012 would have been $1.7 trillion smaller.[5]

How does labor force participation vary across countries?

In almost every country in the world, men's labor force participation is higher than women's, but the increase in women's LFPR is not a phenomenon limited to the United States. Across the globe women have been increasingly entering the labor market, although there is considerable variation across countries.

Figure 1.4 depicts women's LFPR for two points in time, 1971 and 2018, for selected countries that are economically quite similar. These data are from the Organization for Economic Cooperation and Development (OECD).[6] Even these relatively similar countries have different female LFPRs. The last set of bars shows the OECD average.

There are a number of possible explanations for these differences in female LFPR across countries. Of course, the primary drivers of women's work decisions are their own earnings potential, the earnings of their husbands (if they are married), and family obligations. However, variations across countries in institutions, social and cultural norms, and public policies also play an important role in explaining cross-country LFPR differences. Economists think of institutions as established structures that are part of a culture or society. They might include the presence of competitive markets, the availability of part-time and full-time work, and the presence of labor unions. For example, the availability of part-time work and/or flexible schedules makes it easier for women with younger children to join the labor force. Social and cultural norms are rules or expectations of behavior based on shared beliefs within a specific cultural or social group. While often unspoken, these

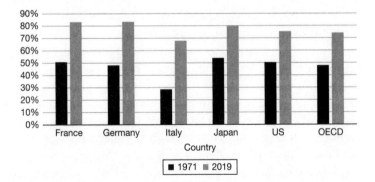

Figure 1.4 Labor Force Participation Rates for Women Aged 25–54, Selected OECD Countries
Source: OECD Database.

norms set social standards for appropriate and inappropriate behavior. For example, in the context of women's LFPR, social norms across the world have long dictated that women should perform unpaid care work—taking care of children and elderly parents, making meals, doing laundry, and other family maintenance activities, for example, while men engage in market work. Public policies refer to rules that might influence labor force participation. Minimum wages and whether or not a country provides paid maternity leave are examples of policies. Paid maternity leave might make paid work more compatible with family responsibilities, so we might expect higher LFPR in countries with this policy.

In the early 2000s, concerned about economic growth, Prime Minister Shinzo Abe of Japan rolled out his well-publicized "womenonomics" plan, aimed at facilitating the entry of women into the workforce. Under this plan, Japan expanded daycare centers, passed a law that limited overtime to 100 hours per month, and expanded parental leave to increase fathers' use of it. This helped fuel the rise in Japanese women's LFPR. Japan was particularly concerned about increasing the number of women in the workforce because historically it has had low immigration rates and an aging population and needed women workers to help fuel economic growth. Unfortunately, many of the women entering the Japanese labor force work in part-time jobs and hence may not be contributing their full potential to the economy. In addition, Abe's plan promised more women in leadership positions, but that has yet to materialize. Entrenched cultural norms about the roles of men and women within marriage and men's obligations to their employers still make it difficult for married women to balance work and family obligations. Japanese men are expected to work long hours and often are obligated to socialize after hours with their colleagues, leaving mothers with primary family responsibilities.

Italy has one of the lowest female LFPRs in the developed world. Somewhat surprisingly, this low female LFPR is coupled with a very low fertility rate—we might expect the opposite, as perhaps Italian women were not working because they were at home taking care of their children. Institutionally, Italy has very strict labor laws that provide job security by making dismissal of employees difficult. Unfortunately, these laws may deter new hiring since employers cannot readily lay people off when demand falls. Additionally, there is little part-time work in Italy, which forces married women with children to decide whether to work full-time or to stay home with their children despite the fact that many women report that they would like to work part-time. Finally, although Italy has a public childcare system, slots are quite limited, resulting in few options for childcare outside the home. Interestingly, the geographic areas within Italy where public support for childcare is low are also the areas with the lowest female LFPR. All of these factors combine to make it harder for women to work in Italy as compared to some other countries.

It is hard not to notice that aside from Italy, the United States has one of the lowest female LFPRs among the countries shown in Figure 1.4. In fact, women's LFPR has stagnated in the United States since about the year 2000. This is not the case in other developed countries such as France, Canada, the United Kingdom, and Japan. All OECD countries have faced similar changes in technology and globalization, suggesting that the answer might lie with differences in labor market institutions. The LFPR slowdown in the United States varies by education. College-educated women have a steady LFPR over this time period, while women with less than a high school diploma experienced a decline in their LFPR. Some of this is due to changes in job market demands that have not favored less-skilled workers. Some speculate that policies such as job search assistance, training, and public jobs programs may help to reverse the trend of lower-educated women's declining LFPR in the United States. A lack of family-friendly policies such as maternity leave and childcare subsidies may also contribute to this pattern. Policymakers and scholars are concerned about this decline in LFPR given the importance of women's labor for economic growth.

Do women work as much as men?

At first glance the answer to this question appears to be obvious. We have just seen that women's LFPR is lower than that of men, although the two have converged over time. But we should not take this to mean that women work less overall than men; as noted earlier, there is a great deal more to work than just work for pay in the formal labor market.

In order to understand work patterns of men and women, we look at data from the American Time Use Survey (ATUS) for working-age adults in the United States.[7] Our analysis of these data shows that although the distribution of paid and unpaid work differs strikingly across men and women, men and women work a very similar number of *total* hours, as seen in Figure 1.5. Whether or not women work less than men depends on the type of work you are talking about. Although women do less paid work per day, they more than make up the

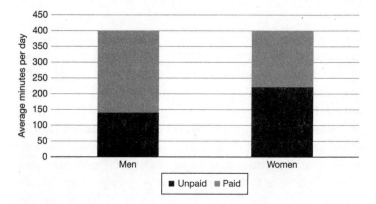

Figure 1.5 Average Minutes per Day of Paid and Unpaid Work, by Gender
Source: 2019 ATUS.

gap with their unpaid work, such as caring for children, shopping, and household work.

Do women take jobs from men?

Sometimes when people talk about women entering the labor market, they express concern that women take jobs from men. This presumes two things. First, that there is a fixed number of jobs, and as we will see shortly, there is not. Second, that the available jobs rightfully belong to a particular group, in this case (white) men. Let's talk about the first issue. Using data from the Federal Reserve Bank, Figure 1.6 depicts total nonfarm payroll (just a fancy way to count the number of people with a job).[8] This diagram shows a positive upward trend in the number of people working since 1948, with employment declines during recessionary periods. It is clear that as women's LFPR has increased, the total number of jobs has as well. As for the second point, no job is an entitlement for any particular group.

Just think about what might happen if women did not work. Economic growth is important to all of us; the size of the economic pie determines how large a slice everyone can have. Without women working, the economic pie would be much

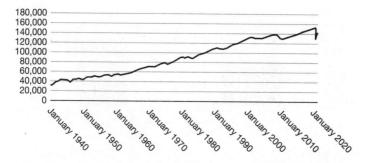

Figure 1.6 Job Growth: Monthly Total Non-Farm Payroll, Thousands of Persons, 1940–2020
Source: St. Louis Federal Reserve Bank.

smaller—we would all be worse off, as less output would be produced.

Does women's work count?

We have stated that women are an important part of the economy and a driver of economic growth. We have also noted that women do a disproportionate share of unpaid work. Measuring women's and men's paid contributions to the economy is relatively easy. Measuring women's (or men's) unpaid contribution is complicated by decisions that have been made about formal measures of economic production, specifically by thinking about "what counts." Most typically, official reports of economic production focus on a measure called gross domestic product, GDP for short.

So, what is GDP? GDP is the primary way we measure and compare how well or how badly an economy is performing. GDP can be described as representing the total value of all the goods and services produced.

When we compare GDP over time within a country, we typically measure it in "real" terms, which is economist-speak for taking out the effect of inflation (or deflation) so that the measures are comparable across years. Because the population can also change over time, we also tend to measure GDP in

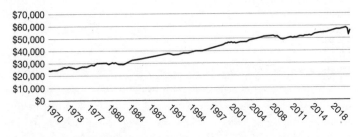

Figure 1.7 Quarterly Real per Capita Gross Domestic Product, Chained 2012 Dollars, Seasonally Adjusted 1970–2020

Source: St. Louis Federal Reserve Bank.

per-capita (the average per person) terms. Figure 1.7 shows real per capita GDP over time for the United States. The good news for the United States is that the trend is positive: the production of goods and services has been increasing for the past half century.

However, for the moment, we are more interested in what is *not* in this measure. GDP does not measure the amount of production from unpaid work—the production of goods and services that are not sold in a market. Some unpaid work is for consumption within the family, such as cooking, gardening, and housecleaning. The products of unpaid work may also be consumed by people not living in the household—for example, cooking a meal for visiting friends, volunteering at a soup kitchen for homeless people, mowing the lawn of an elderly relative, or coaching the local soccer team. This type of work, particularly that done within the family, is often but not exclusively performed by women. Economist Marilyn Waring was instrumental in pushing the awareness of the importance of counting unpaid work as economic activity in systems of national accounting.

But how do we know if unpaid activities are comparable to work performed in the labor market? One way to identify unpaid work is to use the third-person criterion. If a third person could hypothetically be paid to do the activity, it is considered to be work. Cooking, cleaning, childcare, laundry, walking the dog, and gardening are all examples of unpaid work, although increasingly we hire people to do many of these tasks, at which point they count as paid work. On the other hand, someone else cannot be paid to watch a movie, play tennis, or silently read a book on another's behalf, as the benefits of the activity would accrue to the person doing the activity. These activities are not work; they are leisure. As you can see, it is important to make this distinction—not too many people would consider reading a novel and vacuuming a house to be equivalent, even though they both represent unpaid uses of time. But we must be careful about using the idea of the enjoyment of an activity as a criterion for leisure. Many people derive a great deal of personal satisfaction from paid work and enjoy their time spent on the job. The level of enjoyment of the person doing the activity cannot be used as a method of distinguishing between work and leisure.

Unpaid household work constitutes an important component of economic activity. Failing to measure it accurately or at all in official measures of economic output such as GDP most certainly leads to incorrect conclusions about how much work is really being done, and by whom. By not counting the output of unpaid work, GDP simultaneously underrepresents total production and diminishes the contributions of women. To recognize this important work, in 1993 the United Nations recommended that countries introduce domestic production into their systems of national accounts. To date, no such adjustment has been implemented by any country.

So, how might we count unpaid work? We could assign the market price to the actual good produced. For example, there are market prices to purchase an hour of childcare, housecleaning services, or a prepared meal. This is termed the replacement-cost approach since it indicates how much it would cost to replace the unpaid work with a market substitute.

An alternative way of measuring unpaid work is the opportunity-cost approach. This approach values the activity based upon the wage rate that the household member doing the activity could have earned if they were working in the labor force as opposed to engaging in that activity. The underlying assumption is that the household member has forgone some earnings in order to do this household production. For example, if you could be earning $15 an hour working and you are home walking the dog, that work would be valued at the $15-per-hour rate, essentially the market value of your time. That might be close to the hourly rate of pay for a dog-walker. But what if you are a highly paid lawyer and you take your dog for a walk? Is the value of that dog walk really equivalent to what you earn per hour? It is pretty easy to see that the opportunity-cost approach can sometimes egregiously overestimate the value of household production. This is particularly true when the skill differences required for the forgone job and the household production are quite different. It follows, then, that the opportunity-cost method will overvalue the same household work if it is done by highly educated women. And what if the household production is done by someone without a market wage—a retiree, for example? Surely it doesn't have a value of zero. Then the opportunity-cost approach gets even murkier: what is the appropriate wage rate to apply? Of course, sometimes we underestimate the skills needed to conduct household production. Is caring for young children really a low-skilled activity? Just ask a childcare provider about the skill set needed to successfully shepherd a group of preschoolers or infants through their day.

Measuring unpaid work is not simple. Nevertheless, despite a long history of being ignored altogether, and some complications inherent in applying each approach, there are now a number of methods to estimate the value of unpaid work.

How much do women contribute to the economy?

This question consists of two parts. The first is to determine how much women contribute in the form of unpaid work. The second part is to value the production of women in the formal economy.

We begin with unpaid work. The ATUS was developed to understand time use in general, and time spent in paid and unpaid work in particular. Using tabulations of reports from the ATUS regarding how much unpaid work is done and then applying the two approaches discussed earlier yields some estimates of how much unpaid work would contribute to GDP.

One estimate, using the replacement-cost approach, indicates that US GDP would be 19 percent higher. If we used the opportunity-cost approach, GDP would be 62 percent higher. The difference between these two estimates is sizable, just as we predicted it would be. Either estimate makes clear that unpaid work is valuable and that failing to count it understates the true level of economic activity taking place, particularly the work done by women.[9]

The OECD did a similar exercise in 2010 drawing on time-use data from twenty-five developed countries.[10] Across all the countries in their study, women do more unpaid work than men; that's not exactly news, but it is helpful to have it quantified. The bulk of this unpaid work is cooking, cleaning, and caring. As in the United States, the replacement-cost approach yields lower estimates than does the opportunity-cost approach. Although the estimates vary substantially across countries, when we average over countries in the OECD we find that somewhere between one-third and one-half of all valuable economic activity is not accounted for in the system of national accounts.

The second part of the question is how much women contribute to the formal sector. Of course, this is part of GDP, but it is not simple to divide production into that produced by women and that produced by men. The Council of Economic Advisors (a group of economists who work for the president and are charged with offering objective economic advice regarding domestic and international economic policy) has answered a related question. Given that we know that women's LFPR has increased greatly from 1970 to the present, the council asked, how much larger is the economy since women increased their labor supply than if they had not? The council's estimates indicate that women worked substantially more hours in 2015 than they did in 1970. These increased hours accounted for $2 trillion of total production in 2015, an increase of 13.5 percent in the size of the US economy.[11]

Although estimates from the Council of Economic Advisors show the importance of women increasing their labor supply over the last four decades, we still have not counted how much of total output is produced by women. To do this, we conducted an analysis similar to what the Center for American Progress did when they attempted to measure what it would be like to have a day without women working. In 2018, according to data from the CPS, men and women worked a combined 33,383,005,835 hours—over 33 billion hours of productivity for the US economy. Women worked 43 percent of these hours. A similar calculation for earnings reveals that women earned 39 percent of the total labor market earnings in 2018.[12] Think of how much worse off families would be without those extra earnings.

What have we learned in this section? A quick summary suggests two important takeaway points. First, unpaid work is worth a lot of money. This is no surprise to those who do it. Much of this unpaid work (but certainly not all) is done by women. Because it is not counted in national accounting, it is as if this labor were invisible. However, as women move into more paid work (presumably hiring other people to do at least some of their previously unpaid work), work that did not previously count is now included in GDP.

Despite the 1993 United Nations recommendation, unpaid work remains uncounted in official estimates of production around the world. Feminist scholars argue that this exclusion introduces a major bias into economic data that can lead to bad policy and, further, that the exclusion is an intentional form of institutionalized gender bias. Economic statisticians, on the other hand, argue that including unpaid work would actually make GDP less useful for policymaking because the estimates of GDP would be unreliable and harder to compare across countries.

How do recessions affect women?

Recessions are downturns in the economy. The National Bureau of Economic Research (NBER) determines when a recession occurs by observing a significant decline in economic activity that is spread across the economy and lasts more than a few months. Recessions are typically triggered by a negative event, such as the financial crisis that led to the Great Recession (December 2007–June 2009) and the COVID-19 pandemic (which led to a severe economic decline beginning in February 2020). Historically, recessions are shorter than economic expansions, but they can have serious labor market consequences for individuals who are affected.

Though a recession is defined by changes in the amount of goods and services produced (GDP), the impact of a recession is felt by individuals in the labor market. As firms reduce their output, the need for labor falls and the unemployment rate typically rises. The unemployment rate is the ratio of the number of unemployed individuals (those who don't have a job but are actively looking for one) to the total labor force.

During a recession, the size of the labor force (the total of the employed and unemployed) can either contract or expand. If a family member loses a job, other members of the family may look for and take up jobs to help replace the family's lost income. This is called the added-worker effect. This can cause the size of the labor force to expand during a recession. On other hand, if jobs are too scarce, people drop out of the labor force altogether, causing the labor force to contract. These people are called discouraged workers. Discouraged workers don't count among the unemployed because they are not looking for work, and their status can make it look like both the unemployment rate and the labor force are declining during a recession.

In a heterosexual partnership, women are often thought of as secondary earners, a somewhat pejorative term meant to imply that they make their work decisions after their husbands make theirs—they view their husbands' work as a given and then choose to work or not. Hence, women are often observed to be the added worker in a recession to replace lost income if their partners become unemployed.

Each recession is different, but most have been "mancessions" in that male unemployment rises more than female

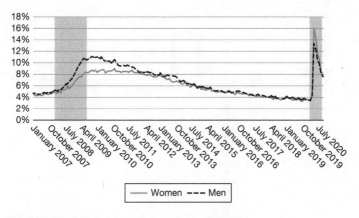

Figure 1.8 Monthly Unemployment Rates, by Gender, 2007–2020
Source: St. Louis Federal Reserve Bank.

unemployment because men tend to work in industries more affected by economic downturns. Women are often in jobs less sensitive to economic downturns, such as education and healthcare. Figure 1.8 shows male and female unemployment rates from January 2007 to September 2020.

During the Great Recession unemployment rose dramatically and male unemployment was far higher than female unemployment. Fast-forward to the pandemic-induced recession that began in February 2020. The spike in unemployment for both men and women is remarkable for how fast it happened. Yet this one is clearly a "she-cession" because women's unemployment is higher than that of men. What's different?

In the pandemic-induced recession, businesses that closed were more likely to employ a larger proportion of women. Those industries include retail, hospitality, non-essential healthcare, and other care work. What we don't see in the unemployment graph (Figure 1.8) is that many women left the labor force entirely due largely to the lack of childcare, school closures, and possibly the need to provide care for elderly relatives. We can see this clearly in Figure 1.9, which plots the monthly change in the LFPR for the year 2020.

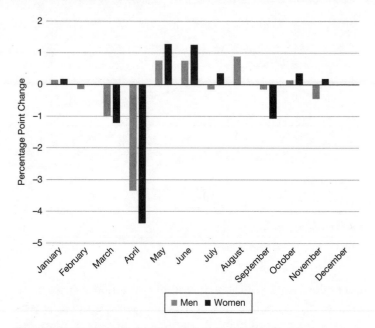

Figure 1.9 Monthly Percentage Point Change in Labor Force Participation Rates by Gender, 2020

Source: St. Louis Federal Reserve Bank.

The drop in labor force participation is acute for both men and women in April and May, but we see a very large drop for women around September—right when online schooling started up again after summer break and parents scrambled to juggle work and schooling. This became necessary because childcare facilities were part of the pandemic shutdown in many states. This had the effect of both leaving parents without childcare services and causing sharp declines in women's employment since childcare centers often had to lay off their (mostly female) workers.

Women of color have borne the brunt of this recession, as they are more likely to work in the previously mentioned industries than white women. Figure 1.10 shows the unemployment rates throughout 2020 for Black, Hispanic, and white

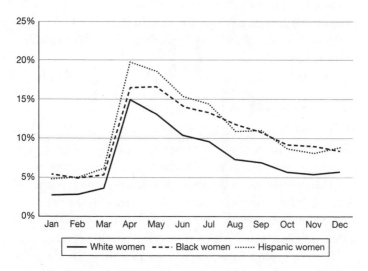

Figure 1.10 Unemployment Rates for Women by Race/Ethnicity, 2020
Source: St. Louis Federal Reserve Bank.

women. The gap in the unemployment rate between Black and white women reaches almost 5 percentage points in August. The unemployment rate for Hispanic women swelled to nearly 20 percent at one point during the pandemic.

Education also played into this recession. Some highly educated women chose to leave the labor force—to balance family and work life—but were able to rely on their partner's income. In contrast, for women with lower educational levels, it was more often the case that their job was eliminated. In terms of job elimination, women who were able to work from home (typically higher-educated women) were more likely to keep their jobs compared to women in industries that required more face-to-face interaction. This division often fell along race and income lines. Exacerbating the problem, lower-educated women who maintained their employment often faced higher health risks due to the pandemic.

The job losses and the related loss in labor market experience will negatively impact women's earnings and hence increase the gender pay gap for years to come. And, of course, the overall future growth of the economy will be negatively impacted as well.

Is women's work different in developing countries?

The United Nations and other organizations classify all countries of the world into one of three broad categories: developed economies, economies in transition, and developing countries. Most of the world's women live in developing countries. A developing country is generally defined as one with a less well-developed infrastructure, a low Human Development Index, and low gross national income.[13] Such definitions are not always agreed upon, and given that there are over 200 countries in the world, one organization's list does not always match another's—this is particularly the case with emerging or transitioning countries, which may straddle two categories. Given the variation across countries, generalizing about women's labor force participation is challenging.

It is probably helpful to start with the big picture. How does economic development relate to women's LFPR? Many economists posit that there is a U-shaped relationship between economic development and women's LFPR. The theory goes something like this. In a low-income country with little industrial development, much of the work is subsistence farming and women are heavily involved. Hence, the LFPR of women is quite high. As the economy develops, an industrialized non-agricultural sector opens with jobs that have been viewed as inappropriate for women in part because they often involve extensive physical labor. These jobs pay more and often pull men out of agriculture and into manufacturing. This typically increases male earnings, which tends to reduce women's labor force participation, because the family becomes better off. As economic development continues, the white-collar sector tends to grow, providing new employment opportunities for women. These jobs typically offer higher pay than agricultural work, and this higher wage draws many women back into the labor force because the price of their time in the labor market has increased. This pattern has been seen in many developing countries but is by no means uniform across countries.

India illustrates this pattern. India, the world's second-most-populous country, has seen its economy undergo structural changes that have influenced women's labor force decisions. For example, India's agricultural sector has become increasingly mechanized and the country has rapidly urbanized, pushing women out of agricultural jobs. At the same time, changes in the manufacturing sector have led to fewer opportunities for women due in part to their low skill and education levels and cultural attitudes about the role of women in these jobs. These developments, coupled with a higher standard of living—which means that many women no longer have to work—have led to a decline in women's LFPR in India since the early 1990s.

China is similar to India in that its economic standard of living has increased rapidly. This higher income means that some families can now afford to have only one earner. And the 2016 relaxation of the one-child policy could mean that families will have more children, which will tend to dampen female labor force participation due to the likelihood of women staying home to provide childcare.

As in developed economies, women who do substantial unpaid work at home are not formally considered workers, and unpaid work by women in developing countries is common and time-consuming. Rather than working in the paid market, women are often engaged in unpaid activities necessary for survival, such as fetching water and collecting cooking fuel. When these activities are combined with caring for young children, it is not surprising that some women find little time to work in the formal sector.

Even when women in developing countries work in the labor market, their attachment to the labor force is often quite different from that of their counterparts in developed countries. Women in developing countries are often relegated to the informal sector, where pay is low and benefits are almost always nonexistent. In this sector, women may work as street vendors, domestic workers, or subsistence farmers, among other occupations. What characterizes these jobs is a lack of protection under labor laws, no pension benefits, and no health insurance. In most developing countries, women make up a disproportionate number of workers in the informal sector.

For women in the Middle East and North Africa, women's LFPR remains quite low, often below 20 percent. In contrast, women in Latin America and the Caribbean have much higher LFPRs, around 50 percent. Still higher are the participation rates of women in sub-Saharan Africa, where 60 percent of women are in the labor force.[14]

Of course, this discussion implies that women are free to choose whether to work and in what occupation. But there may be constraints, in the form of customs or laws, limiting the ability of women to work outside the family farm or other family enterprise. For example, laws may restrict women from working outside the home, as was the case in Afghanistan under the Taliban in the 1990s. Cultural norms may also play a role. The low female LFPR in many Middle Eastern and North African countries often reflects cultural norms such as maintaining a woman's purity.[15]

We've already highlighted that the LFPR of women has been a boon to economic growth. It turns out that there is a synergistic relationship between women's LFPR and economic development. Rapid economic development requires women contributing to production beyond their household. However, it is not until a country develops economically that jobs become available to women in the formal sector, allowing them to make this contribution. This is one of those classic "chicken or the egg" problems—which comes first?

Falling fertility rates and increased literacy and education across the developing world have caused women to work and contribute to economic development. And most developing countries have been growing robustly since the mid-1990s, creating opportunities for women. Yet an analysis of ninety-five countries finds that female workers currently generate about 37 percent of the world's GDP—a number considerably lower than their 50 percent share of the global working-age population.[16] There is still capacity for women-driven future growth.

Do women influence family spending decisions?

In this section, we started out to answer the question "Do women *control* family spending decisions?," but it turns out this is a difficult question to answer with any confidence. Although it has been bandied about in the popular press that women control 80 to 85 percent of spending, it is surprisingly difficult to track down the data source and methodology for this estimate.[17] A *Wall Street Journal* article that tries to locate a source for the data reports wildly varying surveys in which both men and women claim to make the majority of the spending decisions. Economists, including Esther Duflo, the first female economist to win a Nobel Prize in economics, express doubt that such a statistic could be meaningfully estimated.

Instead of relying on difficult-to-verify and inconsistent commercial survey data, we again turn to the ATUS to see if we can uncover men's and women's shopping behavior. These data show that women spend more time shopping than men, both for groceries and for other consumer goods. While the shopping difference is noticeable for single women compared to single men, the gap is substantially larger for married women compared to married men. Among couples, women take on more shopping responsibilities for the family.

While women shop more than men, it is important to consider the distinction between time spent shopping and control of spending decisions within couples. It turns out that this distinction, which may seem only semantic at first, has real consequences for women. Work by economists stresses the important role of "bargaining power" in family decision-making.

A simplistic version of this complicated theory highlights that the partner with greater earning power (and better economic opportunities outside of marriage) has greater decision-making control within marriage. Because men's earnings tend to exceed those of their female partners, men enjoy greater bargaining power and decision-making control within the family. Although increases in women's wages relative to men's may have narrowed the gender pay gap, our calculations from national data indicate that married women under the age of sixty out-earn their husbands in only 25 percent of couples.[18] If this pattern of earnings translates into influence over spending decisions, household decision-making may still be a man's domain.

The conclusion of a number of studies by economists to understand both bargaining power and spending preferences is that greater control of resources by women results in different spending patterns than when the same resources are controlled by men. An interesting example of this is from studies that found that expenditures on women's and children's clothing rose as a share of total family expenditures while purchases of alcohol and tobacco products declined as women's bargaining power increased.[19] In studies situated in developing countries when government programs provide income directly to women in poor families, spending on children's nutrition, education, and health tend to increase.

Is there a pink tax?

The "pink tax" occurs when products that are marketed to women and girls or that have what is perceived to be a feminine look to them have a higher price tag. Here are some examples. One of the authors was giving a talk about this very topic and on her way stopped in a convenience store. Hanging on a rack right next to each other were a package of twelve disposable blue razors, seemingly for men, priced at $4.99, and a package of twelve pink but otherwise identical razors marked at $5.99. In addition, when it comes to basic clothing items such as socks and sweatshirts, there is also a price difference, perhaps hidden by the fact that these products are often displayed in different parts of a store. The pink tax even applies to children's products. In fairness, a quick check online at one store listed pink and blue scooters each priced at $29.99. At another store, they were on sale for similar prices, but the original prices were $50.93 and $39.99 for pink and blue, respectively. Keep in mind that this is not illegal and is not, in fact, charging men different prices than women. If women want to buy blue razors, they can, and pay $4.99 just like male consumers.

These price differences, however, are typically hard to justify. One might think that the cost of producing different products could account for their price differences. But one can hardly imagine that pink plastic (or paint) costs substantially more than blue. There are a few cases in which cost differences have been used to justify gender-based price differences. For example, the posted prices for dry-cleaning and pressing women's shirts are typically higher than the same services for men's shirts. Pressing irons were originally made in sizes more suitable to men's clothing and were designed for cotton fabrics, and so the smaller sizes of women's clothing and the synthetic materials often used in them meant that pressing women's clothing was more labor-intensive. Yet this suggests that pressing large women's cotton blouses should cost less and cleaning small men's shirts made of synthetic fabrics should cost more, which is not often the case.

There are more examples of price differences for goods and services for men and women that might have some underlying justification. Health insurance for younger women is more expensive arguably due to the cost of pregnancy, but shouldn't this cost be shared with fathers? Doesn't the higher risk of dying faced by men at all ages compared to women merit higher healthcare costs for men?

Other arguments have been made to justify these price differences. Maybe women have stronger preferences for product differentiation, and that costs more. This is a common defense among manufacturers and retailers. If women prefer and will pay for having a wider range of hair care products or jeans tailored to more body types, manufacturers will argue that it costs more to produce and stock a larger variety of products. Of course, the very companies that manufacture these goods benefit greatly from women's more diverse preferences; they try to shape these preferences with their marketing to see goods at higher prices and enhance their profits.

Price differences are not necessarily a form of discrimination. The term "discrimination" refers to situations where otherwise equal individuals are treated differently. For example, even when men and women have equal risk profiles, women often pay higher mortgage rates, and yet they default on these loans at lower rates. That example is often cited as price discrimination because the product is the same and women are better credit risks—so why should they pay higher mortgage rates? Another well-known example is auto repairs. Higher prices are often quoted to women for automobile repairs, and this is frequently attributed to the fact that women typically have less mechanical knowledge. Closely related, a clever research experiment, referred to as an "audit pair" study, sent men and women out to purchase automobiles and found that with the same credit rating and negotiating strategies, men were able to purchase cars at lower prices.[20]

There are some products where men pay more than women. Notable among them are automobile insurance, where male drivers have a higher risk of accidents and face higher premiums. Similarly, higher male mortality is reflected in higher life insurance rates. Even without an identifiable cost difference, cover charges at bars are often lower for women because bars benefit from having both men and women as customers. Because some women demand black luggage (the authors of this book both own black carry-on suitcases) but few men demand pink luggage, a pink carry-on is often less expensive than a black one.

It is easy to find examples of the pink tax, but really, how much difference does it make? Enough to matter, that's for sure. A 2015 study by the New York City Department of Consumer Affairs found that, among other products, women paid 8 percent more for clothing and 13 percent more for personal care items.[21] A study of the prices paid for services such as dry cleaning, hair services, and tailoring in California indicated that women paid more than men—over $2,300 more per year at today's prices.[22]

In many cases, it is obvious that these price differences are not justified by differences in the cost of production. That sounds like discrimination. So what can be done? As we noted, it is not illegal to sell a pink scooter at a higher price than a blue scooter. Our advice is to buy the blue scooter and call out the hypocrisy. Mention it to a store manager; ask why there is a difference. Pictures of price differences posted on social media could prompt an important conversation—see #pinktax for examples.

Some states have taken formal steps to try to combat this gender-based price discrimination. The California and New York reports mentioned previously were commissioned precisely out of concern about what was considered an unfair business practice. California enacted the Gender Tax Repeal Act of 1995. Even so, in the more than two decades since this action, goods and services targeting women still cost more, but efforts continue. The Pink Tax Repeal Act was introduced in the US House of Representatives in 2019 (HR 2048). At the time of this writing, the House has yet to take action.

A more targeted campaign has addressed gender inequities in the treatment of health-related products. This is the one example that really does involve a tax. Many medical products are exempt from sales taxes, but such a waiver does not include menstrual products, obviously used by women. Tampons and other supplies are deemed luxury products and subject to sales taxes. Michigan and New York have been sued to eliminate such a sex-based tax, which has been called unfair, inequitable,

2

IS THERE SUCH A THING AS WOMEN'S WORK?

Social norms regarding women's roles have evolved. Throughout history there have been cultural expectations about the division of labor between the sexes. Prior to the Industrial Revolution in the United States, women and men often worked side by side, typically on a family farm or in a family business. After the Industrial Revolution, most men went to work in factories, performing jobs often considered dangerous, dirty, and inappropriate for women, while women had primary responsibility for work done in the home. It is only relatively recently that women, particularly married women, gained more autonomy and reentered the workforce in large numbers. In fact, for much of history, a married woman was considered subordinate to her husband—it was not even until the 1970s that a married woman could apply for credit in her own name. It is not surprising that women's family responsibilities often impact their labor market choices. In this chapter we explore the evolution of gender roles, the types of work that women perform, and social and contraceptive changes that have influenced women's family responsibilities and work choices.

How have gender roles evolved?

The division of labor between genders varies significantly across societies. In some cultures women actively participate in employment outside of the home, while in others there is a clear specialization of tasks along gender lines. These differences are most clearly illustrated by the differences in female labor force participation, which vary widely across the world, from 21 percent in India to 61 percent in Sweden. Gender roles manifest themselves in myriad other ways as well, from business ownership to political representation.

Where do these gender roles come from? This is one of those big-picture questions where no single discipline can claim ownership. Here we look at several examples of how economics has contributed to our understanding of the evolution of gender roles. Ester Boserup, an influential Danish economist, hypothesized that historical differences in how agriculture was practiced played an important role in defining social perceptions of appropriate gender roles.[1] For example, where the soil was hard, a plow was often necessary to break up the soil for planting. The use of plows required a great deal of physical strength, so they were typically operated by men. In areas where the soil was easier to manipulate, women had a larger role in agricultural production compared to areas where a plow was required. When the plow was required there was more specialization in production on the basis of gender: men labored outside in agricultural production, while women typically worked in the household. Boserup further suggested that this specialization, in turn, led to the development of norms and beliefs about appropriate gender roles, beliefs that persisted even after that particular form of agriculture declined and societies became more industrialized.

A careful statistical examination of Boserup's hypothesis linked ethnographic information about preindustrial societies to contemporary measures of a society's norms and behaviors concerning women working in the market sector of the economy and their involvement in politics.[2] The underlying information on agriculture comes from a highly regarded anthropological study on early agriculture, including plow use, for 1,265 ethnic groups around the globe. The study links this information to current gender roles, including women's LFPR; the share of firms that are women-owned, which is a measure of women's entrepreneurship; and the share of seats in a national parliament or other comparable legislative body held by women, which is an indicator of their political power.

The analysis confirms Boserup's hypothesized effect of plow use: in areas with a historical tradition of plow use we currently see lower LFPR of women, fewer women legislators, and fewer female-owned businesses. Who would have guessed that hard soil would determine women's current gender roles as measured by their economic and political standing today? Cultural norms appear difficult to change.

Another example of the way in which the past can influence current gender roles comes from a study of unbalanced sex ratios. Between 1788 and 1868, about 162,000 convicts were transported from Britain and Ireland to various penal colonies in Australia. Most of them were guilty of petty crimes, and only one in seven of these convicts was female. This policy resulted in heavily male-biased sex ratios.

As you might imagine, at this time Australia was a country where women's economic opportunities outside marriage were limited and rather unattractive. For example, women worked doing laundry and cooking, and some even resorted to prostitution to survive. As financial independence was difficult if not impossible to achieve, women would often find themselves better off if they could find a man to marry who would provide for them, even if this man had a criminal history. Such high male-to-female ratios enhanced an Australian woman's opportunities for marriage and likely decreased the probability that she had to work outside the home.

The convicts were initially brought to Sydney, the first European settlement on the continent. Many of the prisoners were subsequently sent across Australia to settle other parts of this vast country. Thus, the ratio of men to women was not the same across the country, meaning that where you lived determined your marriage prospects. The male-biased sex ratio ranged from a low of 2:1 to a high of 18:1. Researchers linked this ratio to several outcomes related to women and their role in society, including the proportion of women married and the proportion of women in the workforce.[3] Did the women who lived in areas with an excess of men have different rates of marriage and labor force participation, as hypothesized? It turns out that this is the case. Women who lived in the areas with very high male-to-female ratios were more likely to be married and less likely to work—consistent with the lack of work opportunities available in Australia to women at that time.

Researchers linked historical data on sex ratios in Australia to the same set of outcomes, marriage and labor force participation, measured in more modern times (2011), as well as an additional outcome: an index indicating traditional gender-role attitudes. Once again, women living in areas where sex ratios had been historically high were less likely to work and were more likely to be married. These women also held more traditional gender-role attitudes. The unintended impact of sending convicts off the Australia in eighteenth and nineteenth centuries cemented traditional gender roles that remain to this day.

Attitudes toward gender roles are also influenced by circumstances related to the gender of one's own children. Does having a daughter (an arguably random event) alter parents' attitudes toward gender roles? In a clever study using British survey data spanning two decades, researchers examined whether rearing daughters changes parental attitudes about whether it is a husband's role to work and a wife's role to stay at home.[4] They report that parenting daughters decreases a father's likelihood to agree with a traditional male breadwinner norm. This is especially the case for fathers of school-age daughters. Further, parenting school-age daughters is associated with a lower likelihood that couples themselves follow a traditional gender division of work. It appears that the birth of a daughter and the subsequent concern about their daughter's interests lead to a change in attitudes among parents. It is possible that such readjustment becomes stronger once their daughters are older and begin to be affected by inequitable gender norms themselves.

Parenting daughters can also alter gender norms in politics. Researchers have examined if politicians who have a daughter or daughters are more likely to vote for policies that benefit women, using US congressional voting-record scorecards created by two women's interest groups—the National Organization for Women (NOW) and the American Association of University Women (AAUW).[5] Both NOW and AAUW, groups focusing on women's issues, score members of Congress on how they voted on legislation of interest to women, including women's equality, health, and reproductive rights. An analysis of congressional voting records indicated that representatives with daughters voted more liberally on women's issues, particularly those regarding reproductive rights.

It is comforting to know that, as shown by studies as diverse as those that examine the impact of physical demands of agricultural work, those that look at changes in the male-female ratio on marriage markets, and those that explore the attitudes of fathers with daughters, attitudes toward gender equality are not immutable. Perhaps more change is on the way.

When was it acceptable for women to work outside the home?

Women have always worked, although much of that work has been inside the home. In many countries, attitudes toward women working outside the home have evolved substantially over time, and there are striking differences across racial groups. Due to the history of slavery in the United States, it has long been considered acceptable for Black women to work. The same has largely been true for immigrant women. However, for white women, particularly those who were married, working outside the home was not viewed favorably—it often implied that the woman's husband could not support her, and this was seen as a failure on both their parts. Social consensus around women working and the weak demand for labor during the Great Depression combined to provide the impetus for enactment of "marriage bars"—literal prohibitions on the hiring of married women into many occupations. These attitudes began to change during World War II with propaganda efforts aimed at drawing women into the workforce to support the war effort (remember Rosie the Riveter). Yet many employers were initially resistant to the idea of hiring women for war work and did so only when the supply of male labor had been completely exhausted because of military conscription, on one hand, and the rapid expansion of demand for labor to produce wartime goods, on the other. Although generally white women with young children were discouraged from working outside the home, tens of thousands of mothers of all races and ethnicities went to work during the war, which displaced them from their positions as the primary caregivers for their children. Government policies were put in place throughout the war in order to retain women in the workforce. For example, the US government operated a far-reaching, heavily subsidized childcare program. This is the only time that the United States has had anything close to universal public childcare and was made possible through the Lanham Act of 1941, which directed federal funding to government-run childcare centers so that women of all incomes could work to support the war effort.

A majority of the women who went to work as part of the war effort hoped to remain in the workforce when the war ended, as evidenced by a survey by the Women's Bureau in Detroit. Despite this preference, at the end of the war thousands of women were told that they were no longer needed, and they were sent home so that men could return to their jobs. This forced exit did not sit well with many women, and some picketed their former employers. The United Auto Workers even held discussions about how to balance the rights of women with the rights of veterans. Economic forces were not on the side of the women, however. The postwar economic boom of the 1950s increased earnings, which allowed families to have one breadwinner—male, because women simply did not earn as much as men, even in the same jobs. The postwar baby boom that accompanied men's return from the war led to a rise in birth rates at the same time that funding for the Lanham Act, which had provided childcare to support women's work effort during the war, ended.

In addition, according to feminist scholars and historians, there was a concerted if subtle campaign aimed at facilitating women's shift to a housewife identity. Historian Stephanie Coontz states that women were advised to return to their duties as mothers and wives (notably, working-class white women and women of color did not have this luxury). Television sitcoms such as *Father Knows Best* and *Leave It to Beaver* helped normalize the idea of the (white) American woman as a housewife. The postwar economic boom increased homeownership and the purchase of new appliances and ushered in a new emphasis on cleanliness in the home. Women's magazines focused articles on recipes and decorating, further stressing the important role of women in the home and encouraging plenty of housework to occupy women's time. All of this helped cement the idea that the rightful role of the woman was back in the home focusing her energy on her family. As noted earlier, long-standing cultural norms resist revision.

Although these noticeable changes in women working during the war were widespread, the general public was slow to embrace the idea that women should work outside the home once the war was over. Evidence for this comes from the General Social Survey (GSS), which has been collecting data about attitudes toward women working outside the home since 1977. In that year a substantial majority of Americans shared the traditional view of men as breadwinners, as reflected by their agreement with the statement "It is better for a man to work and a woman to stay home," although as Figure 2.1 shows, this view has since eroded.

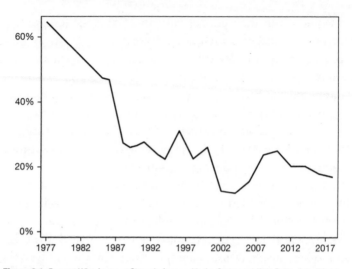

Figure 2.1 Percent Who Agree or Strongly Agree with the Statement "It Is Better for a Man to Work and a Woman to Stay Home"

Source: 1977–2018 General Social Survey.

As public opinion toward women's work and equality of economic opportunities has changed, the debate surrounding women's work and its implications for family and children has risen to the forefront. In 1977, two-thirds of Americans surveyed in the GSS believed that "preschool kids suffer if mother works," but by 2018, just under 20 percent held this view. In addition, in 1988, about one-third of GSS respondents believed that "family life suffers if mom works full time," but by 2012 just under 20 percent felt that this was the case.

So where did these changes in attitude come from? At the turn of the previous century, women, particularly white married women, derived their identity from their work at home. However, over time, as the economy evolved, women's identities did as well. As we've seen, World War II played a role in changing the thinking about the contributions that women could make to the workforce. And men eventually became more accepting of their wives working, though not immediately.

As time went on, changes in birth control technology further allowed women to begin to see their futures not just as wives and mothers but as labor force participants. With this new ability to plan the timing of their children, women sought out more education, going to college in increasing numbers and entering graduate programs that required enormous up-front costs. They began to anticipate careers rather than just jobs. As these events unfolded, attitudes changed dramatically, as shown in Figure 2.1.

How did women progress from jobs to careers?

Women's relationship with work, especially paid work, has changed over time. From the late nineteenth century until at least the 1920s, working women generally did not think of themselves as having careers—and, quite frankly, neither did society. Because most women anticipated working for only a short time before marriage and starting a family, they did not prioritize their education. Exacerbating the situation was the fact that many institutions of higher education were not even open to women. Thus, although women held jobs, these were not long-term professional commitments that would be considered careers.

Things began to change as more of the population completed high school (including women) and as advances in technology (e.g., typewriters and duplicating machines) increased the need for clerical workers and this work became acceptable for women. These jobs required only a high school diploma, and many of the women who filled them may have viewed them not as careers but rather as a way to support themselves when they were single or earn extra money for their families.

Starting around the 1930s and continuing through about the 1950s, the LFPR of married women began to increase substantially. Bars against married women working had begun to lift, and more part-time work was available. Survey data indicated that society began to relax its negative views of married women working outside the home. Advances in household technology such as refrigerators and washing machines also freed up women's time and facilitated their entry into the workforce—although it's possible that the reverse is true, that the needs of working women may have fueled the development of these new technologies. It would be a stretch to define the jobs that most women held at this time as careers, although many did enter professions such as teaching and librarianship. It was still expected that the husband would be the primary breadwinner, and married women were most often secondary earners who made work decisions in response to family needs.

Through the 1990s married women's LFPR continued to rise. With high school diplomas in hand, and increasing educational opportunities available, married women found work in varied occupations as teachers, nurses, social workers, and librarians. These professional jobs looked more like careers, but unlike professions dominated by men, they usually offered limited opportunity for advancement. Many married women did not expect to be employed most of their lives and hence made decisions about their field of study and occupation based on family roles and expectations.

Prior to the 1970s, women married early enough that their adult identity was formed after marriage; hence they viewed themselves primarily as wives and mothers. However, this changed following the 1970s, as women married later and began to invest in education targeted toward a career. As a result, an important part of their identity was also their role at work. They were also more likely to go to graduate school, a sign that they envisioned working throughout much of their adult lives. This was doubtless also due to increases in the availability of birth control, which allowed women (and their partners) to time and space births more accurately. By the end of the 1970s, women were increasingly in careers. For example, in 1960 only 7 percent of lawyers and judges were women, but in 1998 that figure was closer to 30 percent.

Economist Claudia Goldin has traced this arc over the twentieth century for college-educated women. She characterizes
women who went to college in the early 1900s as having to
choose between having a career and having a family. It simply
was not possible to do both. Those who attended college
around the time of the Great Depression often had a job first,
then later a family. Those who attended in the post–World War
II era, through the mid-1960s, had a family first, then a job.
Those who attended during the mid-1960s to the late 1970s
had the career-to-family progression, and those going to college after 1980 combined career and family concurrently.

What jobs do women perform and how has that evolved over time?

There are jobs that people commonly thought of (and largely
still think of) as "women's work." It likely will not surprise
readers that a quick online search of nurse Halloween costumes
predominantly yields images of girls in white skirts wearing
stethoscopes. A number of years ago a similar search for doctor
Halloween costumes would have resulted in costumes for
boys; today that search today produces a mix of both boys and
girls in scrubs or white coats and stethoscopes. Yet a search
for mechanical engineers results in images nearly exclusively
of men working with heavy equipment. Differences in the
types of occupation held primarily by men and women are not
rooted in a single, simple explanation but are related to many
factors, including the attitudes of employers as well as individual choices, traits, and skills. These views, thankfully, continue to evolve.

The social view of women as workers, and the types of
work they do, transformed throughout the last century. In
fact, women's ability to work in certain occupations faced a
number of early social and legal impediments. Notably, a 1908
Supreme Court decision (*Muller v. Oregon*) upheld an Oregon
law that prevented women from working more than ten hours

per day in "mechanized" establishments, significantly less than the amount of time allowed for men. This ruling has been described as "enshrining the primacy of women's domestic roles and defining all women as potential mothers and housekeepers for the good of the nation."[6] Clearly these views have shifted in the ensuing century, but women's underrepresentation in traditionally male-dominated occupations seems to change slowly.

The separation of genders by occupation, what economists refer to as occupational segregation, remained high and relatively stable in the United States from 1900 through the 1940s, when World War II marked an entry point for many women into jobs traditionally held by men. Augmenting a depleted workforce, these working women convinced the public that women could perform a wide range of jobs, from assembly lines to management. Thankfully, from our perspective, the separation of women and men by occupation has been declining over recent decades, yet there are occupations that even today are perceived as "women's work," while others remain stubbornly dominated by men.

As a rather ironic example, there appears to be almost no reduction in occupational segregation among PhD economists.[7] When the authors earned their PhDs in the early 1990s, just about 30 percent of economics PhDs were granted to women—a percentage that is little changed today. The proportion of women in economics departments at universities is substantially lower than 30 percent and falls as professorial rank rises—less than 15 percent of economists at the highest rank of full professor are women.

To investigate the gender composition of occupations, we examine occupations that are perceived to be dominated by men or women. It is common to default to feminine pronouns when describing teachers, nurses, librarians, and social workers. These occupations are often viewed as an extension of the caring roles women take responsibility for in their homes. By contrast, doctors, lawyers, professors, and managers are more likely assumed to be male. Are these stereotypes accurate? Let's take a look.

It comes as no surprise that this segregation is rooted in history. Women were overrepresented in teaching, nursing, librarianship, and social work eighty years ago. Indeed, nearly three-quarters of all female college graduates in 1940 worked in these fields. By 2002, less than 30 percent of all such women worked in these fields. In contrast, only about 13 percent of women college graduates worked in professional occupations such as physician, lawyer, professor, scientist, and manager in 1940. This proportion had reached nearly 50 percent more than six decades later.[8]

Table 2.1 presents recent data on earnings and occupations. Occupations are ordered according to the percentage of female employment, from lowest to highest. We can see that in the occupations that are predominantly male, in the top rows

Table 2.1 Percent Female Employment, Median Earnings, and Gender Pay Ratio for Full-Time Year-Round Workers Aged 25–64 in Select Occupations

	Percent Female	Women's Median Earnings	Men's Median Earnings	Women's Earnings as a Percent of Men's Earnings
Physicians	38.4%	$181,826	$252,536	72.0%
Managers	40.3%	$69,700	$90,913	76.7%
Lawyers and judges	40.7%	$111,116	$141,420	78.6%
Professors (all post-secondary)	48.3%	$65,659	$75,761	86.7%
Elementary teachers	80.2%	$52,528	$56,568	92.9%
Social workers	81.1%	$50,506	$48,487	104.1%
Librarians	82.2%	$53,538	$60,609	88.3%
Registered nurses	86.3%	$66,864	$71,930	93.0%

Source: 2019 ACS.

of the table, median earnings for both men and women are higher than in occupations that are predominantly female. A common tool for comparing men's and women's earnings is using a statistic that represents women's median earnings as a percentage of men's. We see in the last column of Table 2.1 that women's median earnings as a percent of men's median earnings in each of these male-dominated occupations is far below 100. For example, the median earnings of female physicians are only 72 percent of those of male physicians. Similarly, in occupations that are predominantly female, shown in the lower portion of the table, in all but social work men still out-earn women. In these female-dominated occupations, the ratio of median women's wages to median men's wages is much closer to 100 (and hence to parity).

These statistics illustrate the pattern for select occupations, but of course there are hundreds of occupations and perhaps some that are not as segregated by gender. To understand occupational segregation by gender overall, researchers typically refer to the "index of dissimilarity," which calculates the proportion of women (or men) who would need to change occupations for the distribution of men and women to be the same across all occupations. An index of dissimilarly of 50 percent indicates that half of all workers would have to change jobs to attain equal gender representation in all occupations. In general, data show that women are increasingly entering previously male-dominated occupations. The index of dissimilarity has declined over time, from 70 percent in 1972 to its current level of about 50 percent, due largely to the movement of women into traditionally male occupations, rather than the reverse.[9] Interestingly, occupational segregation is lowest for highly educated men and women. It is only 40 percent for college graduates, compared to nearly 60 percent for those who did not graduate from college.

There are a number of possible explanations for the persistence of occupational segregation. One is that men and women have different preferences for types of job and sort themselves accordingly. For example, a number of studies have shown that, on average, women have different attitudes toward competition and risk than men. Analysis from a detailed database that links job attributes to occupation documents a sharp reduction in the proportion of women in occupations that have a high "competitive index."[10] This general finding is supported by many detailed studies of women's occupational choice.

Another difference in preferences that affects job choice is the desire to make a "social contribution" through one's job by actively helping people. The importance of social contribution is often measured by responses to questions about how important it is to be service-oriented or to assist or care for others. To measure the possibility that the social value of one's work might matter, occupations can be ranked by their social contribution. Occupations that are predominantly female, such as nurse and social worker, score high on this measure. The proportion of women in an occupation, which in part reflects women's values, increases sharply as the social contribution index of the job increases.

Men and women bring different skill sets to their work, so it would not be surprising to see gender differences in occupations along these lines also. For example, the proportion of women in an occupation declines the more physically demanding the work. In contrast, as interpersonal interactions on the job increase, the proportion of women in the occupation rises. Somewhat less obviously, as the importance of cognitive skills on the job increases, the representation of women is higher, but only slightly.

In addition, many women seek out jobs that provide workplace flexibility. Evidence shows that occupations with greater scheduling flexibility and less rigid demands on the number of hours worked are associated with a higher proportion of women. This finding is certainly a reflection of the increased family responsibilities taken on by women and particularly mothers.

Despite increased gender integration in the workplace, sub-stantial occupational segregation remains. Perhaps the most important question is: does occupational segregation between genders matter? The answer is almost certainly yes. Gender sorting into different occupations translates into striking differences in earnings. Traditionally, as women entered career fields in large numbers, these occupations became marginal-ized in terms of both status and pay. In the early 2000s, among the twenty-five most common occupations, those made up of more than 70 percent women had median earnings of just over $36,000. In contrast, occupations more than 70 percent male had median earnings of nearly $50,000.[11]

Perhaps because of the history of pay differences in occupations dominated by women or due to perceptions of the masculine identity associated with men's work, the feminiza-tion of certain occupations is not due exclusively to women en-tering predominantly male occupations; a contributing factor is men fleeing them after enough women enter. Evidence for this comes from the occupation of bank teller, where the pro-portion of men in this position declined from over 80 percent in 1930 to under 20 percent by 1970. Similar but less dramatic declines were found in occupations such as ticket agent, news vendor, insurance agent, and typesetter. This so-called tipping-point phenomenon is observed in areas where sexist attitudes are more prevalent and may also explain why integration of occupations has been slow. This pattern of sorting, where women are overrepresented in lower-paying occupations, is a major contributor to overall gender pay differences.

How are gender differences in occupation related to women's family responsibilities?

Family responsibilities disproportionately fall to women, al-though the reasons for this are not well understood. Is it that women care more about families and children? That women are better suited for work at home and with children? Or that women have had fewer opportunities in the labor market and so give up less to assume extensive family responsibilities? In this section we briefly explore these questions and discuss the interrelationship between family responsibilities and women's occupational choices.

Though we know that women spend more time in family- and child-related activities than men, there is no clear way to assign the cause of this pattern to women's preferences versus other factors. There are a number of attempts to gain insight from surveys designed to reveal individual preferences.[12] First-year college students were asked to identify the factors that are important to their personal satisfaction. During the 1960s men were nearly 25 percent more likely than women to identify financial success as being essential or very important to their personal satisfaction; on the other hand, women were over 10 percent more likely than men to identify having a family as being essential or very important for their personal satisfaction. By 1980, the gap in the importance of families had closed, and female and male first-year college students in this survey were equally likely to identify having a family as being very important. This suggests that over the last four decades, at least for well-educated young women, a greater importance placed on a family is not the driving factor in women continuing to take on disproportionate family responsibilities.

Although Figure 2.1 demonstrates that fewer and fewer Americans think that men should work and women should stay home to take care of families, someone still has to take on the responsibility of childcare. Women's lives change substantially with the birth of a first child. Clearly the impact of pregnancy falls on biological mothers, and childbirth necessarily leads to an interruption in work behavior. Once the child is home, though, mothers and fathers could share responsibility for childrearing equally. However, this is not typically the case.

A recognition that family responsibilities can lead to interruptions or reductions in work suggests that women may value flexible work schedules. In addition to occupational segregation across gender, we also see striking patterns in the occupations chosen by women with children. Women with young children are overrepresented in psychology (particularly school psychology), preschool and elementary education, nursing, and physician assisting. School psychology and teaching afford mothers a yearly work pattern that matches up with the school year (presumably one experienced by their children). In addition, nurses and physician assistants are often able to choose more flexible schedules, like a four-day workweek or afternoon or evening shifts if desired.

Pharmacy has also been identified as a particularly family-friendly occupation with flexible work scheduling; this despite the fact it requires advanced education. The flexibility is due in no small part to changes in technology that made it easier for several pharmacists to serve the same customer with no reduction in the quality of service. Unlike our interactions with a physician or an attorney, most of us are perfectly happy picking up our prescriptions from whichever pharmacist is on duty, and we increasingly receive our medications via mail. Hence, forming a relationship with a particular pharmacist is no longer a necessary part of the transaction—indeed, many people do not interact directly with their actual pharmacist at all. This makes it easy to substitute different pharmacists so that female (and male) pharmacists can enjoy more flexible hours. It is not surprising, then, that the profession of pharmacist has become increasingly female. Compare this to hiring an attorney to represent you in court. It is very likely that you care quite a bit about who represents you and that you are not willing to entertain random substitutions. This makes the profession of trial attorney relatively inflexible.

The evidence indicates a disproportionate presence of mothers in family-friendly occupations. Because educational preparation is necessary for (at least some of) these occupations, women must make a series of interrelated choices. Not only do they choose jobs that are complementary to raising a family, but for some women this may require planning an education trajectory long before they have a family.

Was World War II really a watershed for women's work lives?

You often hear that World War II (which occurred between 1939 and 1945) was a defining event that permanently changed women's attachment to the labor force and helped usher in a new era regarding the acceptance of women in the workplace. You may also hear, however, that when men returned home from the war, many women went back to their domestic lives, leaving some to argue that this was a temporary change. So what really happened with women's work lives after World War II?

We all know the war took a toll on the predominantly male soldiers who went to the battlefields. But what was happening on the home front initiated important social changes for women. Between 1940 and 1945, the male labor force declined by almost 9 million and the female labor force increased by 7 million. This increase in women's work can be attributed both to the reduction in available male workers and to the expansion in demand for labor needed to produce military hardware to support the war effort.

If the war was truly a watershed, we would expect that women who worked during the war would continue to work afterward. Yet this was not always the case. For example, over half of the white women between the ages of thirty-five and sixty-four (likely done with their childbearing) who were working in 1950 had also been working in 1940; in other words, they worked before the war. And of those who entered the labor force during the war, a substantial percentage were no longer working in 1950. From this vantage point, the war does not appear to be a watershed event for women's LFPR.[13]

To dig deeper into this pattern, it helps to look at how men were mobilized during the war. Depending on military needs, many men who worked in certain agriculture and war-industry occupations were able to receive deferments. In states with fewer deferments more men left for the war. This created a greater need for women to take over jobs that were vacated. On average, 46 percent of all men aged eighteen to forty-four were mobilized across the United States, but this ranged from a low of 40 percent to a high of around 56 percent. In states with high mobilization rates, more women worked.

Not surprisingly, some women were affected by the wartime job market more than others, depending on their education and their marital and family status. Work behavior by women who had not finished high school was essentially unaffected by mobilization rates. Women who had finished high school had a different response, which varied by their marital status. Among high school graduates, single women and married women without children in high-mobilization states worked more than their counterparts in low-mobilization states. The LFPR of married women with children was unaffected by differential mobilization rates across states because their husbands, as fathers, could receive deferments from military service. These effects continued even after the war, providing support for the idea that the war was a watershed event in women's LFPR.[14]

World War II also affected the types of work that women did. Prior to the war, very few women worked in blue-collar jobs. Manufacturing was considered dirty and dangerous and hence unsuitable for women. But the war effort provided unprecedented opportunities for women to make inroads into historically male-dominated occupations. Some women left school and began working in these blue-collar jobs, which paid well relative to the typical jobs that women (even educated) women would have held at the time. But did this occupational shift persist into the post–World War II period? For the women who were of working age during the war, yes. They continued in blue-collar work, although certainly some were displaced by men who returned home. However, the cohort that came after, who were not yet of working age during the war, entered the workforce in clerical and teaching occupations rather than continuing the increased presence of women in blue-collar jobs.

How did birth control and abortion affect women's work and family trade-offs?

We have seen that women's family responsibilities affect their work and occupational choices. Although various types of contraception have existed for centuries, prior to reliable and accessible means to control fertility, when a woman married, she had a great deal of uncertainty about when she would start a family. And an unmarried woman faced even greater uncertainty about her future by having sex outside of marriage. In short, a lack of reliable contraception or access to legal abortion meant that a sexually active woman did not have complete control over her work and family choices. An unexpected pregnancy was a relatively common event, and even women who might not have been planning a family often chose jobs and education that would accommodate the possibility of family responsibilities. If an unmarried woman found herself pregnant, she typically married the father in what came to be known as a "shotgun" marriage. Investing in education that would lead to a longer-term career typically did not pay off for women, as their plans could easily be derailed by an unplanned pregnancy.

The advent of effective birth control and the legalization of abortion have allowed women to better plan both their reproductive lives and their economic lives. In 1999, *The Economist* called the birth control pill the "the most important scientific advance of the twentieth century." As recently as sixty years ago, contraceptives and information on contraception were considered obscene and banned under federal and many state statutes. In addition, abortion was illegal. In 1957, the birth control pill was introduced, but initially only as a means to control menstruation. In 1960, the birth control pill was approved for contraceptive use. It was the first form of birth control that separated contraceptive technology from the act of intercourse. Prior to 1976, the pill was generally available to married women, but unmarried women and minors did not enjoy the same access. Abortion was not legal until the 1973 *Roe v. Wade* decision.

At the time the pill was initially introduced, women typically married around age twenty and men around age twenty-three. Since then, there has been a steady rise in both men's and women's age at first marriage: in 2019, women's average age at first marriage had climbed to twenty-eight years and men's to thirty years. Hence, the introduction of the pill and access to legal abortion certainly seem to correlate to a higher age at first marriage. The same pattern is true for women's education and labor force participation, which increased significantly over the 1960s and the 1970s.

Differences in women's ages, their marital status, and their state of residence determined when they had access to the pill, and this variation helped researchers understand the impact of the pill on choices women made regarding marriage, fertility, and the labor market. Not surprisingly, this research indicated that the introduction of the pill led to increases in women's (and men's) education and career investments, as women were more likely to work for pay, invest in on-the-job training, and pursue traditionally male professional occupations. These investments paid off as women's wages rose relative to men's. One estimate indicates that the shrinking gap between men's and women's earnings in the 1990s can be attributed to changes made possible by the pill. Although women delayed childbearing, many women eventually had children—they just did so on their own timing.

Although the pill was more effective than other methods of contraception available at that time, it still had a 9 percent failure rate if not used correctly, and hence access to abortion was also important for women even if they responsibly used contraception. The effects of the pill may have been partially offset by the fact that more teens and women were having sex (it was, after all, the sexual revolution of the 1960s), and so birth control failure, although relatively low, affected more people. The legalization of abortion in 1973 also made it possible for young women and teenagers to avoid early marriage and motherhood and hence make long-term investments in their education, which changed their labor-market-related decisions. One estimate is that legal abortion reduced the shotgun marriage rate by 63 percent and also caused a 19 percent reduction in births, particularly first births, which fell by over one-third. These are not inconsequential changes in women's lives.[15]

The advent of the pill coupled with legal access to abortion has provided women much more control over the timing and spacing of their children, allowing them to map out their family and work trajectories and to be more strategic in the kind of education and career path they choose. Rather than being limited to a certain narrow set of fields such as nursing and teaching, they now can make long-term investments in their education, knowing that these investments can pay off in their futures. For example, today half of law, medical, veterinary, and dental degrees go to women. In some sense, women became more like men in that they had much more control over the trajectory of their own lives, which allowed them to enter occupations that required more commitment to the workforce. It is clear that the way women with families interact in the workplace has changed dramatically with improved access to contraceptive technology.

3

HOW DO WOMEN BALANCE WORK AND FAMILY?

It remains true today that women provide a disproportionate share of unpaid household work around the world. Much of that time is spent in the care of children, which requires parents to balance work at home and in the market. In this chapter we start by exploring the gender division of labor in the household for both same-sex and opposite-sex couples. We also examine how couples "bargain" over dividing their time between unpaid household work and work in the labor market. Because marriage and childrearing had traditionally interrupted (or ended) women's careers, we describe the extent to which the allocation of time at home still tilts toward women and impacts their economic lives. We also explore the role of technological change in shaping women's time allocation. We close the chapter with an examination of policies that aim to help women (and men) balance their work lives with family obligations.

What is the gender division of labor within a household?

Within households, women still perform more of the unpaid caring work. Data from a survey in the United States called the American Time Use Survey (ATUS) makes clear a sizable gender gap in unpaid household and caring labor (caring labor encompasses both childcare and eldercare), as shown in Figure 3.1.

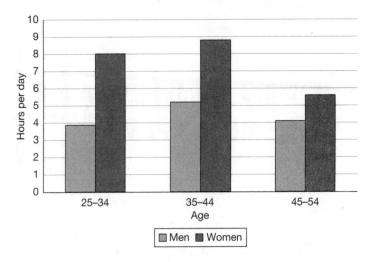

Figure 3.1 Hours per Day Spent on Unpaid Household and Care Work in the United States by Gender and Age Group

Source: IWPR Analysis of 2018 ATUS data.

This gap is largest between the ages of twenty-five and thirty-four, which is the peak childbearing period.

From gender-specific breastfeeding demands to the care of preschool-aged children (which can be done by either parent), the reality is that women take on more of this unpaid work. When children begin attending school, that frees up some parental time, yet women still tend to be in charge of shuttling their children to team practices, music lessons, medical appointments, and other out-of-school activities. Furthermore, when schools closed during the 2020–2021 COVID-19 pandemic, mothers emerged once again on the front lines of caring for children and households.

Unpaid household labor varies by women's labor force participation and education. Perhaps not surprisingly, women who work full-time spend less time per day (4.9 hours) on unpaid household and care work compared to women who are not in the labor force (6 hours). Although women with a college degree and women whose highest level of education is a

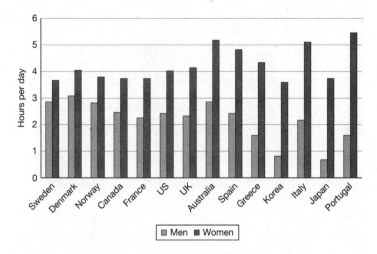

Figure 3.2 Hours per Day Spent in Unpaid Care Work by Gender for Selected Countries
Source: 2019 OECD employment database.

high school diploma do similar amounts of household work (5.8 and 6 hours per day, respectively), the same is not true for men. Men with a high school diploma do 3.5 hours per day of unpaid and caring work, while college-educated men do 4.1 hours per day.[1]

The gender gap in caring and unpaid household work is not limited to the United States. Data from other developed countries reveal similar large gaps, as seen in Figure 3.2.[2] The bars in the figure are arranged by the size of the gap in hours, from smallest to largest. Nordic countries have the smallest differential, while Japan and Portugal have the largest gap in unpaid care work hours per day.

The gender gap in unpaid care work is even larger in the developing world. By region, these differences range from two to ten times more unpaid household and caring work by women than men, as shown in Figure 3.3. In North America, women spend 4.2 hours per day in care work, while men spend 2.7 hours, resulting in a gap of 1.5 hours. The gap is more than double that in regions that include many developing

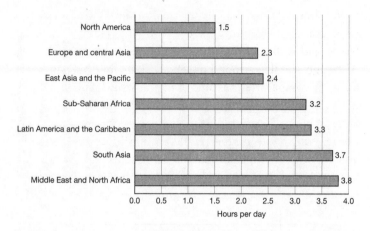

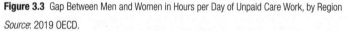

Figure 3.3 Gap Between Men and Women in Hours per Day of Unpaid Care Work, by Region
Source: 2019 OECD.

countries, such as the Latin America and Caribbean region and South Asia.

How do couples decide who does what?

A family unit often provides a place where partners can share work both in the market and at home. Ideally there is an allocation of paid and unpaid work that generates the most income and home production for the family and reflects both partners' preferences. So how exactly do couples make the time allocation decision?

Economists developed models of specialization that involve figuring out who has the "comparative advantage" in different types of production. The simplest model splits work into two types, work in the labor market and work at home. Comparative advantage refers to identifying the partner who is best at earning in the market or working at home while giving up the least. Let's take an example of a couple with young children in which the wife is trained as a surgical nurse and has experience in cooking and childcare. Her husband, in this example, is a long-haul truck driver, is an exceptional cook, and is great with the kids. Both have labor market and household skills, though the wife has greater earning power. Although she has strong household skills, her husband may have the comparative advantage in household work and gives up relatively less in market wages by specializing in unpaid work at home. This could result in nearly complete specialization, in which one partner works primarily in the household and the other in the labor market. Complete specialization has become less common in recent decades but still occurs in some families when children are still young. In 2019, among married couples with children, one-third had only one parent working in the labor market. Given the gender pay gap and the fact that men may have fewer domestic skills, it is more likely that the man works in the labor market and the woman has the comparative advantage in household work.

As families decide on an allocation of market work versus household work and family caregiving responsibilities, an economist would suggest that one important consideration is the opportunity cost of the caregiver, as in the example just given. Women, who traditionally earned less than their husbands, were the natural choice to care for children, as less income would be lost by their reduced labor supply. However, it is increasingly common to see women in professional jobs (almost a quarter of all working women out-earn their husbands). Despite this phenomenon, and although men have begun to take on more family responsibilities, stay-at-home fathers are still far fewer than stay-at-home mothers—often regardless of the differences in their incomes. Sometimes opportunity cost considerations seem to conflict with more traditional gender roles.

Of course, work allocation decisions may involve more than just who can produce more effectively at home or give up less in the labor market. Individuals may view working in either the labor market or the household as intrinsically rewarding based on their individual preferences, so the decision about who does what also hinges on who has more decision-making power in the relationship. This leads us to economic models of household bargaining. Early models of household decision-making presumed that an altruistic "household head," assumed to be the man of the house, made all decisions for the good of everyone in the family. That 1950s-style representation of how households operated was exemplified and simplified by television shows, advertising, and long-standing, culture-based assumptions. Eventually, the recognition that this was not an accurate portrayal of how family decisions were made prompted the development of household bargaining models.[3]

Though often mathematically complicated, household bargaining models have intuitive appeal in explaining how couples make decisions that consider the preferences of both partners. Partners bargain over decisions such as who will take out the trash today and where to go on vacation as well as bigger decisions about the division of work in the market and unpaid housework during their marriage. Perhaps paradoxically, an individual's bargaining power within their relationship has a lot to do with their alternatives outside of the relationship. That is, if an individual can earn a high salary in the labor market or has ownership of valuable assets such as property or inheritance, they could afford to live alone without a partner, which gives them greater weight in decision-making within the marriage. Similarly, if there is an abundance of potential alternative partners, then an individual would also have greater bargaining power within their marriage. Consider when there are many more men than women in a "marriage market." Women have a far wider range of choices, and a woman would choose a partner who grants her greater decision-making power.

So how does this play out? Trying to measure whose preferences are driving decisions in marriage is not easy. There is, however, research suggesting that in households where women have greater bargaining power, often measured by higher education and wealth or earning possibilities, outcomes seem to line up with women's preferences. Birth rates tend to be lower, reflecting women's lower desired number of children; the division of household work tends to be more equal; and spending on items directly consumed by women and children tends to rise. In general, studies show that women's assets and opportunities outside of marriage increase their bargaining power and more equal division of work inside their marriages. In the most extreme cases, domestic violence against women is lower in partnerships where women have higher bargaining power.

Because the actual earnings of men and women within a family are not exclusively measures of bargaining power but also outcomes of the bargaining process—that is, women with greater bargaining power can and do spend more time in the labor market and therefore earn more—it can be difficult to measure true bargaining power and its impact on family decision-making. In light of this difficulty, there are many examples in the research of different ways in which bargaining power is measured. As a starting point, studies using education as a signal of a woman's earning power (and hence her opportunities in the labor market) illuminate a simple pattern: the gender gap in household work is substantially lower—though not eliminated—for educated men and women. But changes in education levels take a long time to evolve. There are other, quicker ways that bargaining power may change.

Control of financial resources is thought to be a powerful contributor to bargaining power. The general thinking is that transferring income to women in families, and mothers in particular, increases their bargaining power and leads to a pattern of expenditures that benefits the family overall. Indeed, the International Monetary Fund has identified the improvement of women's property rights and their ability to own assets as an important step toward gender equality. In fact, in one of the main messages from its 2012 report, the World Health Organization said that "greater control over household resources by women can enhance countries' growth prospects by changing spending patterns in ways that benefit children." This line of thinking led a number of international agencies to provide targeted transfers and lending programs for women in developing countries, to further this end and benefit the next generation.

A change in household spending in response to income transfers targeted to women seems to occur in developed countries as well. One notable research study examined a cash transfer to families with children in the United Kingdom in the 1970s. This child benefit payment started out being provided to the family as a whole but later was provided specifically to mothers. The shift in transfers resulted in increases in expenditures on items benefiting women and their children (primarily women's and children's clothing).[4] It should be noted that providing the child benefit payment directly to mothers was viewed by at least some members of Parliament as a slap in the face to men. It was clear that the control of this additional income, which strengthened the bargaining position of these women within marriage, posed a threat to men making decisions for the whole family. Economic models of bargaining power seem to have captured an important— and sensitive—aspect of family dynamics: control of family finances.

Bargaining power within the family is also affected by opportunities in the workforce. In particular, as women's wages rise relative to men's, women's relative bargaining positions improve. Does such a shift in bargaining power translate into changes within families? To answer this, one study used changes in demand for goods and services in California that differentially affected occupations with predominantly male or female workers.[5] As an illustration of such a change in demand, take the service industry, which is dominated by women, and the construction industry, which is dominated by men. If the demand for new construction dropped tremendously and the demand for services remained unchanged, men's earnings would fall relative to women's and this would increase women's bargaining power. Examining the impact of such changes in the relative wages of men and women on domestic violence reports reveals a striking pattern: as women's earnings increased relative to men's, hospitalizations resulting from domestic violence declined. Similar studies examining the impact of gender differences in unemployment in the United Kingdom find similar results (but in reverse): as women's unemployment spikes, domestic violence increases. As the economy moves through recessions that differentially impact women's versus men's employment—including the 2020 COVID-19-related recession—household bargaining models suggest that the consequences can be serious.

Other factors determining bargaining power go beyond the labor market. Some studies focus on the "marriage market" or opportunities for other relationships. For example, unilateral divorce laws that allow women to end an unhappy marriage without the consent of their husband reduced the incidence of domestic violence within marriage. Increases in the male-to-female sex ratio (the number of men relative to women—an indicator of the availability of alternative male partners) also increase the bargaining power of women. As women's bargaining power increases by virtue of more possible partners, the gender balance in unpaid household work improves. Data from China (where the sex ratio exhibits a lot of variation over time and across provinces) indicate that as the ratio of men to women increases and women have more bargaining power, the gender gap in time spent cooking, cleaning, and in childcare narrows.[6]

Is the division of labor different for same-sex couples?

Presumably, gay and lesbian couples feel less bound by culture-based norms regarding gender roles within a household; hence, they can exercise more leeway to determine how they wish to divide their time between unpaid household and market work. So, are same-sex couples as likely as opposite-sex couples to have one partner who takes on the majority of the home and family responsibilities? Data collection has been slow to catch up with the realities of modern family life. For example, the ATUS data, while allowing identification of sexual orientation by respondents, nevertheless collects time-use data from only one member of each household, which means that measuring specialization within a couple is not possible. The ATUS does, however, collect data on non-market time use, which allows for a comparison of patterns of time use for cohabiting gay men and lesbians and for their heterosexual counterparts.

One study using these data reported that, on average, gay men living with a partner spent more time in household work than married heterosexual men. This difference persisted even when considering other factors that could explain differential time use, such as age, education, and partner income, and the effect is larger in families where children are present. For the most part, after accounting for these factors, there were no differences in time spent on household labor between partnered lesbians and either married or unmarried cohabiting heterosexual women. Women seemed to perform household work in keeping with their gender roles, regardless of their sexual orientation. Because heterosexual women are partnered with men who are performing less unpaid work at home, this pattern suggests that far more unpaid work at home is accomplished in lesbian households.[7]

Without data on both partners in a household, the ATUS cannot be used to fully answer the question at hand. To address this gap in the data, psychologists conducted smaller surveys of lesbian and gay couples regarding their work at home and in the labor market in order to compare with heterosexual couples. The first study compared reports of thirty-three lesbian couples with children to the same number of heterosexual parent couples. Though not asked in the same fashion as a time use survey, both parents in each couple reported the percentage of household and childcare tasks that they typically performed, on a scale ranging from "I do it all" to "My partner/spouse does it all." Their answers served as scores for their involvement in unpaid household work. The survey also included questions regarding employment status, hours worked, and individual income. The results of this study indicate that lesbian couples tend to divide paid market work and unpaid childcare time more equally than heterosexual couples, although there was no (statistical) difference in the division of non-childcare household work.[8] A more recent (and larger) survey focused on the division of labor of gay fathers and similarly reported an egalitarian division of unpaid household labor and childcare.[9] One very recent study examined the division of labor for transgender and non-binary (TGNB) parents. The researchers' analysis of a relatively small sample size finds that TGNB parents are also generally egalitarian in the division of their unpaid household and childcare labor.[10]

Of course, specialization in unpaid household work is risky. If the partnership dissolves, the individual who specialized in household work may have difficulty finding employment and supporting themselves. Marriage confers a sense of long-term commitment reinforced by a legal arrangement that is costly to dissolve. With this increased sense of permanence, partners are freer to invest in the relationship, including specializing in unpaid household work. This raises a follow-up question: have same-sex couples taken advantage of the legal commitment afforded by marriage to have one partner fully specialize in household work?

The history of same-sex marriage is short. In 2004, Massachusetts became the first state to legalize same-sex marriage. Thirty-seven states and the District of Columbia followed suit. On June 26, 2015, the US Supreme Court struck down all state bans on same-sex marriage, thus legalizing it in all fifty states, and also required states to honor out-of-state same-sex marriage licenses.

The advent of marriage equality did not mean that same-sex couples had not been cohabiting prior to these legal changes. Indeed, the American Community Survey (ACS) a survey conducted annually by the Census Bureau has provided estimates of the number of same-sex couples annually since 2005. In 2010, when same-sex marriage was still illegal in most states, data from the ACS estimated that there were 150,000 married same-sex partners and 440,000 unmarried same-sex couples. By 2019, the number of married same-sex couples had increased to more than 568,000 (slightly more women than men), with another 411,000 same-sex cohabiting couples. As we would expect, the advent of marriage equality precipitated a sharp rise in the proportion of same-sex couples who were legally married. In 2010, 26 percent of same-sex couples were married, and by 2019, nearly 58 percent of same-sex couples were married—a percentage greater than that of opposite-sex couples.[11]

As the marriage equality movement gathered support, states legalized same-sex marriage at different times. Comparing the time allocations of same-sex couples in states that passed marriage equality laws to those in states that did not, both before and after legalization, allows us to learn about the impact of the institution of marriage on time allocation. While gay men made no change in their paid work hours, lesbians reduced their annual hours of paid work in response to marriage equality, and women who had lower earnings than their partners decreased their hours of paid work the most. How did they spend their time out of the labor force? Time-use data show that lesbians reallocated work hours mainly to unpaid care labor. These results indicate that marriage rights likely increased specialization among lesbian couples.[12]

How did technology change the work women do?

In 1900, the average woman between the ages of twenty-five and fifty-four spent over 50 hours per week in household production; the average man of that age spent 3.7. By 1950, this gap had narrowed, but not substantially; women's average work time declined to 42.7 hours and men's increased to 9.2.[13]

From 1950 to the present, total time spent in unpaid household work has not declined substantially, and although the gender gap continues to narrow, women still spend far more time on household work than men.

Near the turn of the twentieth century it took a considerable amount of time to sustain a household. For example, as detailed in a research article, in 1890, the absence of running water and central heating meant that the average household had to manually handle and transport seven tons of coal and nine thousand gallons of water annually. Even washing clothes was an elaborate and time-consuming ordeal. One had to bring water to heat on a wood- or coal-burning stove, and the clothes were cleaned using a washboard or mechanical washing machine. Then the garments were rinsed, the water was wrung out by hand or a mechanical wringer (no spin cycle), and the clothes were hung out to dry on a clothesline. Clothes often had to be ironed using heavy irons heated continuously on the stove. In the early decades of the twentieth century, household technology across the board was primitive by current standards. Barely one-fifth of US households had central heating, flushing toilets, and electricity, and less than half had running water.

In 1912, interviewed by *Good Housekeeping* magazine, Thomas Edison foretold a dramatic change in women's lives: "The housewife of the future will be neither a slave to servants nor herself a drudge. She will give less attention to the home, because the home will need less; she will be rather a domestic engineer than a domestic labourer, with the greatest of all handmaidens, electricity, at her service."[14]

Have Edison's predictions come true? In the mid-1940s one housewife described her time spent doing laundry before the adoption of electric washers, dryers, and irons. Using this old technology, it took her 4 hours to do the wash and another 4.5 hours to iron it. By 1980, with the new technology, it took 41 minutes to do the wash and 1.75 hours to do the ironing—clearly a time-saver.[15] Technological developments of the sort foretold by Edison certainly have changed the nature of household work and greatly reduced the amount of time it takes. Spurred by technological development, unpaid work in the household today looks very different from 1900, but the one constant is that women do much more of it than men.

Did this change in technology alter the gender gap in housework time? The first half of the twentieth century saw the rapid diffusion of electricity into homes across America. From that point forward, the invention of (and inexpensive access to) home-focused time-saving technology such as washing machines, vacuums, dishwashers, and the more recent microwaves and even Roombas suggested that dramatic decreases in time spent in unpaid work at home were possible. The reduction in the value of household work time almost surely contributed to women's increased labor force participation. Using a variety of techniques and data, analyses produced a range of estimates suggesting that household technology afforded women greater opportunities to participate in the labor market. These estimates ranged from 10 percent to 50 percent of the increase in women's labor force participation (with the larger effect occurring during the first half of the twentieth century, when new technologies such as refrigerators and washing machines were adopted).

Technology made unpaid work at home easier and reduced the gender gap in labor force participation. Although technology reduced the time necessary to minimally maintain a home, time spent in unpaid household and care work is still substantial and disproportionately performed by women.

How is the timing of births related to a woman's career?

Most women in the United States will be mothers at some point in their lives. For example, in 2014, 85 percent of forty-five-year-old women in the United States had given birth. Given the time-consuming nature of raising children and the fact that nearly 60 percent of women are in the labor force, what does this juggling act look like? Do women more often have children at the beginning of their careers or after they are established? Do most working women take leave to care for children or continue uninterrupted? There is no simple answer to these questions. In fact, the two authors of this book, both mothers, chose very different paths. One of us had two children during graduate school, while in her twenties, and the other had two children in her thirties, just before and after earning tenure. Though the timing worked for both of us and we continued successfully in our schooling and careers, we acknowledge the challenges that we faced as professionals raising young children.[16]

Women have increasingly delayed motherhood; the average age at first birth in the United States has increased from twenty-one in 1972 to nearly twenty-seven in 2018. Not surprisingly, this delay has been accompanied by a reduction in the total number of children a typical woman has. As reported by the World Bank, the total US fertility rate declined from 2.01 to 1.73 over the same period, now well below the replacement level of 2.10.

Note that within that average, there is a wide variation in the age when women begin to have children. Though, as noted, the average age at first birth is about twenty-seven years, an increasing number of first-time mothers are over the age of thirty-five. Age at first birth varies substantially by the characteristics of mothers. Asian women wait, on average, until age 30.5 to have their first child, Black and Hispanic women on average have their first child at age 25, and Native American women initiate motherhood at the youngest age, 23. The patterns by education level are equally striking. The average age at first birth for women with a college degree is over the age of thirty (30.3), while women with lower levels of education have their first birth nearly seven years younger (23.8).

Can women successfully combine breastfeeding and work?

The American Academy of Pediatrics recommends exclusive breastfeeding for the first six months of an infant's life. Many studies establish positive correlations between breastfeeding and beneficial outcomes for children. But mothers who breastfeed are not a random sample of all mothers; statistically, they have higher levels of education and are more likely to be married. In addition, they may also engage in other behaviors that benefit their children, which makes it difficult to sort out the effects of breastfeeding from other parental inputs to children's well-being.

Short of running an experiment where some infants are randomly assigned to breastfeeding while others are not, an approach that is not likely to be ethically sound, economists have had to resort to other techniques to separate correlation from causation. A promising approach has been to compare siblings, one of whom has been breastfed and one of whom has not. Assuming the only difference between the siblings is breastfeeding, comparing siblings allows the researchers to control for other hard-to-measure family factors, both background and environmental, that may influence the decision to breastfeed and be related to the outcome under study. Such sibling studies have found benefits of breastfeeding for infant health and cognition, although the benefits are smaller than the correlational studies have reported.

The Centers for Disease Control (CDC) releases a biennial breastfeeding report card. Statistics for babies born in 2017 indicate that about 25 percent of mothers exclusively breastfed for six months, although 84 percent reported at least some breastfeeding. This is an improvement from a decade earlier, when about 11 percent of new mothers breastfed exclusively for six months and 74 percent reported some breastfeeding.

Why are the rates of exclusive breastfeeding so low? For a very few women, it is simply biologically not possible. Others are just not interested. For some who wish to breastfeed, a quick return to work and lack of workplace accommodations for nursing mothers can make breastfeeding a daunting if not impossible task.

To assist women with breastfeeding, the 2010 Patient Protection and Affordable Care Act (ACA) mandated that private health insurance plans provide support for breastfeeding, including lactation consultants and breast pumps. Because this ACA mandate was only in place for mothers with private health insurance, this situation provided a setting very much like an experiment, where some mothers had a new opportunity for support services while others remained without. This change in the law was not related to any one mother's decision to breastfeed, so it was somewhat like a randomized trial. Comparing those mothers who received the increased support to mothers whose health insurance was through Medicaid (which did not provide the additional support) revealed that this intervention was found to increase rates of initiation of breastfeeding, most importantly for groups that typically have lower rates—women of color and women with less education.

The return to work is not simple. The American College of Obstetrics and Gynecology recommends that women take at least six weeks off after the birth of a child, but 25 percent take less than that, which makes the continuation of breastfeeding much more difficult. When women do return to work, they often reported having to pump breast milk in appalling conditions—sometimes in the restroom while seated on the toilet! The ACA requires employers to provide a nursing mother reasonable break time to express breast milk and a place to do so. Certain companies, including Google, Marriott International, and Cisco Systems, have received accolades for their accommodations. These companies and many others supply private, quiet, well-furnished spaces for women to pump breast milk. But at the present time monitoring the implementation of the law is difficult, and it is hard to know how many firms have complied.

While there is no magic solution for increasing the rate of breastfeeding, the practice is on the rise in the United States. Experts attribute this to public health campaigns that make mothers aware of the benefits of breast milk for their babies, as well as support for new mothers that makes it easier for women to combine work and breastfeeding. The statistics indicate, however, that we are not there yet. One estimate suggests that exclusive breastfeeding for the first six months of an infant's life could save the United States $10.5 billion in healthcare costs annually.

How does women's work behavior reflect family responsibilities?

Raising children is costly. In addition to the out-of-pocket costs of childbirth and all of the material needs of children—for example, their food, clothing, toys, books, and schooling—a huge portion of the cost of children is the time that it takes to raise them. This time can be provided by many people—mothers, fathers, extended family, and paid childcare providers are all possibilities—but it is indisputable that much of the time commitment is met by mothers.

How does this time commitment by mothers fit with their market work? The traditional version of motherhood and work followed a predictable pattern. Figure 3.4 shows the age profile of women's labor force participation at different points in the last seventy years. Using Census data from 1950, 1960, and 1980 and data from the ACS in 2000 and 2019, we see a striking change over time. In the 1950s and 1960s, an M-shaped pattern of increased labor force participation in their teens and early twenties, with sharp decreases from age twenty through their early thirties, reflected women exiting the workforce during typical childbearing years. Though some of these women entered (or reentered) the labor force in their forties, women of the 1950s and 1960s never fully returned to the initial, pre-childbearing LFPR. By 1980, we see dramatic increases in LFPR

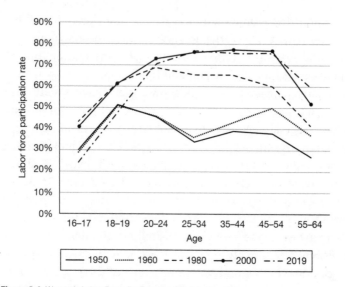

Figure 3.4 Women's Labor Force Participation Rates by Age Group
Source: BLS.

for women of all ages and, importantly, a much smaller decline potentially associated with childbearing. By the year 2000, the M-shape has completely disappeared; women's LFPR rose nearly continuously with age until retirement. Nevertheless, mothers are twice as likely as fathers to indicate that parenting interferes with career advancement.

So have women stopped altering their market work when they become mothers? We saw that occupational choice is impacted by women's family responsibilities, as some mothers choose occupations such as nursing, teaching, and pharmacy because they offer the possibility of more flexible hours, part-time work, and the ability to leave and reenter the workforce without career setback. This suggests more nuanced impacts of children on a mother's work than simply whether she leaves the labor market or not.

Data from the Current Population Survey (CPS; the same survey used to calculate the official US unemployment rate) indicates that women are three to five times more likely than men to voluntarily work part-time between the ages of twenty-five and fifty-four. To what extent is that related to women's increased responsibilities for children?

Figure 3.5, panels A and B, show women's work status (not working, working part-time, or working full-time) for married women aged twenty-five to forty-five by the presence of minor children and the age of their youngest child. Panel A shows work patterns for college graduates, and panel B shows patterns for women with less than a college degree. There are a number of things to consider here. First, these work patterns are shown for married women. Even without children, these women have some family responsibilities, and when they have children, presumably they can work together with a spouse to decide whether and how much each of them will work to financially support their family and how much time each will devote to childrearing.

Beginning with panel A, a few things are striking. In general, most married college-educated women work, and the majority work full-time. Part-time work is most predominant for women with young children. Full-time work increases steadily with the age of the child but is highest for those with no children (74.1 percent).

Panel B reports the work status of married women with less than a college education. Similar to married women with a college education, absence from the labor force is most common for women with the youngest children and full-time work increases as children age. Because these women's earnings are lower, the opportunity cost of reducing work hours to care for children is lower for this group and is reflected in these numbers. A comparison of panels A and B makes it clear that the level of full-time work is always higher for college-educated, married women.

Although not shown, the patterns for unmarried women are similar. These women are more likely to have sole responsibility for childcare and for providing for their family's

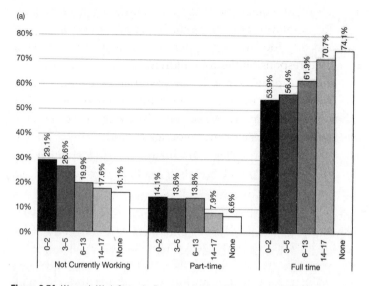

(a)

Figure 3.5A Women's Work Status by Presence and Age of the Youngest Child, Married College Graduates

Source: 2017–2019 CPS.

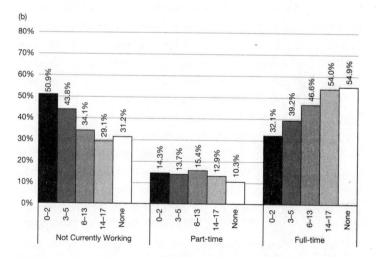

(b)

Figure 3.5B Women's Work Status by Presence and Age of the Youngest Child, Married Non–College Graduates

Source: 2017–2019 CPS.

financial needs, and so they are more likely to work than married women regardless of the presence and age of their children. Like married women, more-educated single women are more likely to work than their less-educated counterparts.

When does the caring end? Women in the sandwich generation

The short answer to the question of when women's caregiving ends is that it doesn't. Women have historically provided care for family members (both children and the elderly). Recent patterns of later marriage and childbirth, coupled with later launching of adult children and increased longevity, have resulted in what has been called the "sandwich generation"— adults with a parent aged sixty-five or older and either raising a child under the age of eighteen or financially supporting a grown child. Women in this generation face an increased likelihood of caring for both children and parents simultaneously. Women baby boomers, who made great strides in educational attainment and participation in the labor force are, in general, healthier, wealthier, and more independent than women of earlier generations. Despite these advances, many women over the age of forty now face the increased caring responsibilities as part of the sandwich generation.

The Pew Research Center reports that in 2012, nearly half of adults in their forties and fifties fit the definition of the sandwich generation. Fully 15 percent of these adults are providing financial support to *both* an aging parent and a child. Adult children have long provided assistance to their aging parents, but what is a newer phenomenon is the degree to which these adults also provide significant support to their children at the same time.

Financial support from the sandwich generation to their parents and children can cause financial strain, but the responsibilities do not stop there. Aging parents increasingly need assistance with daily living, and while the provision of financial assistance impacts both men and women, it is women who predominantly provide both emotional support and hands-on assistance for children and older parents. Caregiving for two generations, which takes time away from the labor market and often involves increased expenses, takes a toll on caregivers through financial and emotional stress. A survey of such sandwich-generation caregivers indicates they report lower levels of financial stability than similar adults without dual caregiving responsibilities, as well as more emotional stress, which manifests itself through health impacts (e.g., an increased incidence of high blood pressure and depression). On the flip side, however, adults who provide assistance to their children and parents may do so because it is intrinsically rewarding; a higher proportion of sandwich-generation caregivers report being generally happy with life as compared to their non-caregiver counterparts (31 percent to 28 percent).

You might think that the caring ends here, as these baby boomers are now aging out of "sandwich responsibilities" and entering older adulthood themselves. Ironically, the caring responsibilities for sandwich-generation women may continue beyond the point where parents no longer need in-home care and adult children fully become independent. Typical age patterns within marriage and gender differentials in life expectancy and morbidity mean that women often provide care to aging husbands experiencing declining health and these women often spend many years living alone as they age. In addition, a new sandwich generation is emerging as adult Generation X children (primarily daughters) are now increasingly assuming caring responsibilities for their parents and children, much as the baby-boomer generation did before them.

Not surprisingly, as baby boomers have aged, commercial living and assisted-care facilities for seniors have proliferated. Increasingly, adult children and their parents can make decisions about living together or near each other while children provide personal assistance to parents or purchase such care in a variety of forms. Senior-care services and facilities can reduce the time commitment of adult children, but the responsibility for care work still falls disproportionately on women, as they constitute the majority of senior-care employees. Such occupations pay substantially less than comparable work. In addition, like childcare and household services, senior-care jobs are often filled by women who have migrated to the United States. Across the United States, nearly one-quarter of direct care workers are immigrants; in some states female immigrant workers make up nearly 50 percent of those in direct care occupations. Needless to say, an evaluation of immigration policies is necessary at precisely the time when expanding the senior-care workforce is paramount.

How do employers and the government help with work/life balance?

Given the dramatic increase in the labor force participation of mothers, there has been increased policy attention to how firms and the government can and should accommodate the needs of working mothers and their families. In the United States, more than 60 percent of children from two-parent families live in a family where both parents work, and 76 percent of single mothers work.[17] Combining work and family can be challenging for parents because the way we think about families and work still revolves around a model of a married heterosexual family with a wife who cares for children so that her husband is free to meet, travel, and/or work at any time without having to worry about his family.

Pregnancy and childbirth almost certainly entail some time out of the labor force for women. Most developed countries provide maternity leave, and some also provide access to other types of leave: paternity (designated for new fathers), parental (available to both new mothers and new fathers), or family (taken to care for ill family members and/ or new children). Most of the time, such leave is taken by mothers around the birth of a child. Unpaid leave forces families to make decisions regarding trade-offs between adequate family income and time spent with children; this may be particularly difficult for low-income families. A survey conducted by the Pew Research Center reveals that 60 percent of individuals with household income less than $30,000 reported that the loss of income while on maternity leave led them to take on more debt, put off paying bills, or even go on public assistance.[18]

Following the birth of a child, most women who intend to return to work must find some sort of childcare. Such care is expensive. In 2018, the average cost to provide center-based childcare for an infant in the United States was estimated to be $1,230 per month. A family with the US median income of $68,703 would spend 21 percent of their income to cover the cost of childcare in a center—three times what the federal government defines as affordable childcare (no more than 7 percent of a family's annual household income). Childcare is typically one of the biggest items in the family monthly budget. It is often higher than the cost of housing, transportation, food, or college tuition (yes, you read that right—in some states childcare is more expensive than college tuition). Some relief is provided in the form of tax credits and subsidies to eligible families.

Why, you might ask, should a family's private decisions about childcare be subsidized by the general public? A fair question. While one might be tempted to see children as something akin to a family pet, providing enjoyment and happiness to the family in which they are raised, children are far more than that. The ability of our economy to support an aging population in retirement depends on maintaining a stable population and the future well-being of our economy depends on an educated and creative labor force. In this way, children are everyone's concern. You need only think about the life-altering contributions of former children such as Susan B. Anthony or Margaret Sanger to appreciate this argument.

The 2020 COVID-19 pandemic highlighted the importance of childcare—its absence has disrupted parents' work, particularly that of mothers. Between August and September 2020, 865,000 women left the labor force. Helping women (and men) balance their market work with their family lives means that women are better able to retain their jobs, increase their earnings, and build their careers. In the next sections we focus on both maternity leave provisions and childcare subsidies—the backbone of policies aimed at helping families balance work and career.

What parental leave policies does the United States have and how do they compare to other countries' policies?

The Family and Medical Leave Act (FMLA), signed into law in 1993, provides families with up to twelve weeks of unpaid leave to care for newborn or newly adopted children or ill family members by guaranteeing return to the same job or level of job. Because of various eligibility requirements (including firm size and length of time a woman has been with an employer), only about 60 percent of the US workforce is covered by the FMLA; some firms provide longer leave for employees, and some provide paid leave. Only two countries in the world have not yet legislated some type of paid family leave: the United States and Papua New Guinea. In many European countries such leave has been in place for decades. Figure 3.6 shows the number of weeks of paid maternity leave for selected countries.

The generosity (percent of salary replaced) of maternity leave varies widely, as seen for selected countries in Figure 3.7. For example, the United Kingdom provides thirty-nine weeks of leave and replaces 30.1 percent of a woman's salary while she is on leave; simply put, women receive roughly the equivalent of twelve weeks of full-time pay during those thirty-nine weeks. Spain, on the other hand, replaces 100 percent of a woman's salary, but only for sixteen weeks.

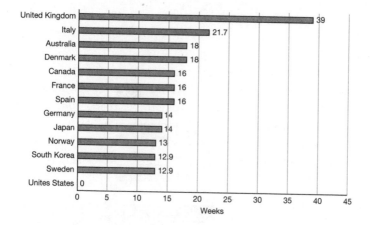

Figure 3.6 Weeks of Paid Maternity Leave by Country
Source: 2018 OECD.

Maternity leave is the most common form of family leave—both in terms of what is offered and what is used. In countries that offer parental leave, women are the main users. Only Sweden and Norway approach parity in the percent of leave taken by men (45 and 39 percent, respectively).

Because the US government has been slow to offer any sort of paid leave, states have begun to fill the void. Prior to 1993, only twelve states had legislated unpaid maternity leave. As of the writing of this book, eight states and the District of Columbia now mandate paid family leave. The average maximum benefit is $1,000 per month, and the leave duration is typically twelve weeks. Eligibility for these paid leaves varies by state.

All of this means that the benefits of family leave depend on a woman's job, the size of the firm where she works, how long she's been employed by that firm, her usual number of hours worked, and her state of residence. These eligibility criteria create inequities in access to leave after childbirth. Evidence suggests that, all factors considered, access to leave is better for

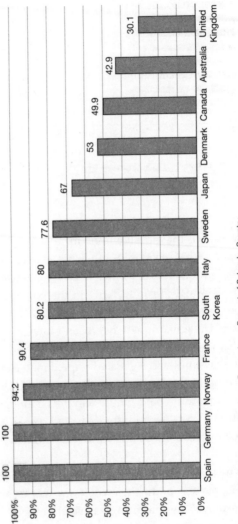

Figure 3.7 Average Maternity Leave Payment as a Percent of Salary by Country
Source: 2018 OECD.

middle- and upper-class families compared to families at the lower end of the income distribution.

What are the economic arguments for mandating leave?

One economic argument predicts that the market will provide the leave that families want, with no role for the government (at least under very specific circumstances). Here is how that argument goes. When hired, employees are typically offered a benefits package that may include maternity leave, healthcare, and a retirement plan in addition to salary. As long as the total costs are the same, employers are indifferent to the exact mix of this compensation package. Employees will then choose the employer that offers the wage/leave combination that fits best with their preferences. Employees who value family leave will have to accept lower wages in exchange for such leave. Under conditions in which employees have complete information about the offers of different employers, and employers have perfect information about the proportion of employees who will take leave, no government intervention is needed—or so the economic argument goes.

In contrast, one argument for mandating family leave is the presence of something called adverse selection. When a woman is hired for a job, she knows if she plans to take maternity leave, whereas the employer typically does not have this information (and it is certainly not acceptable for the employer to ask). Unlike the conditions specified in the first argument, where both sides have perfect information, economists call this difference in information "asymmetric information." This asymmetric information can lead to adverse selection in the following way. Women who anticipate using family leave will try to obtain jobs at firms that provide such leave. Firms offering leave will have higher costs because they will attract all the employees who want family leave, and these firms will have to deal with costly disruptions that result from employees taking this leave. Therefore, market forces will discourage the voluntary provision of leave by firms. Mandating that all firms provide such leave evens the playing field and is a simple solution to the problem of adverse selection.

Provision of leave also generates "positive externalities"—benefits that accrue not just to the leave-taker and their family but to society as a whole. Enabling a parent to be home with very young children leads to beneficial health outcomes for children, including improved birth outcomes, reductions in chronic conditions, and fewer hospitalizations. The provision of leave has also been found to improve the mental health of mothers. The presence of such externalities adds to the justification for mandating family leave.

What are the consequences of providing leave?

Here we consider five possible behavioral reactions to the provision of leave: the change in the probability of taking leave itself (take-up) and the effects on women's earnings, employment, fertility, and breastfeeding. The research on each of these topics is abundant and ongoing as new data become available and economists come up with innovative ideas for how to identify the causal effects of maternity leave policies.

Take-up

It may be surprising that individuals, particularly fathers, do not always take leave when it is available. Onerous eligibility requirements and the absence of job protection for those women not eligible for the FMLA may inhibit women from taking leave. In one survey, more than half of women not taking leave, particularly low-income women, said their reluctance was because they worried about losing their job. Even so, implementing new maternity and family leave policies or extending existing policies has been shown to increase leave-taking.

Earnings

A key feature of the FMLA is that it guarantees the leave-taker the right to return to her pre-birth employer in the same job (or one at the same level). Taking leave from her current employer, rather than quitting and starting again, allows a woman to continue to build work experience with her current employer and helps keep her earnings on their original trajectory.

The positive effect of leave-taking on women's pay may be offset if the leave is for an extended period of time and a woman's human capital depreciates. This can be particularly important in industries where keeping up with new developments is paramount—think of the technology industry. A year off from such a job can disadvantage a woman a great deal, as new platforms may emerge that will render her previous skill set at least somewhat obsolete. The same effect occurs in other occupations as well, though not necessarily as acutely. Although results from studies examining short leaves are mixed, research from many countries suggests that particularly long leaves can be detrimental to women's earnings. Clearly more research is needed to fully understand the impact of leave on women's earnings.

Employment

Access to family leave may also affect a woman's employment decision. A woman who considered dropping out of the paid labor force upon giving birth might find that the leave is long enough for her to feel comfortable taking leave and returning to her employer, hence maintaining employment continuity. Some high-profile companies such as Google and Accenture report that their turnover rate for new mothers fell when they increased available leave. However, studies in countries that provide for particularly long leaves report some declines in women's long-term employment and career advancement.

Fertility

Many European and Asian countries experiencing low fertility have turned to enhanced family leave and other work/ life balance policies to increase fertility. The theoretical impact of leave on fertility is ambiguous. On the one hand, it lowers the opportunity cost of childbearing for working women. On the other hand, if it increases labor force attachment, it may reduce future childbearing given that the opportunity cost of having a child rises with the length of time a woman has been in the workforce. It is not surprising, then, that evidence on the effectiveness of parental leave policies on increasing fertility is inconsistent. Nevertheless, countries continue to include increased leave among their pro-natalist policies.

Breastfeeding

Providing leave may also improve child health by facilitating breastfeeding. Several studies have used the 2004 implementation of California's paid family leave program (the first in the nation) to study just how this can happen. Since the decision to breastfeed is not random—we saw earlier that married women and women who are college graduates are far more likely to breastfeed exclusively—simply comparing breastfeeding rates before and after a change in a family leave program won't tell us much about causality. In something akin to an experiment, however, women in California after the implementation of paid leave were found to increase breastfeeding relative to similar women at the same time in neighboring states without paid leave.[19] Another study used this method but looked at both California and New Jersey (which implemented paid family leave in 2009) and found policy effects that were larger for more educated mothers— who are already more likely to breastfeed.[20] Perhaps the leave payments are insufficient to support low-income workers who cannot afford wage losses.

Who helps families meet their childcare needs?

Families raising children can care for their young children themselves, use paid childcare providers, or make other arrangements such as enlisting relatives to care for their children. Some two-parent families stagger their work schedules so that one parent can be home at all times—an option obviously not available to the approximately 25 percent of single-parent families with children under the age of eighteen. The United States lacks a well-developed set of policies that address affordability of and access to childcare. States and employers have filled some of the gaps.

Before we launch into what the United States provides, we note that most developed countries provide government-subsidized childcare, and some are quite generous. For example, although school isn't mandatory in France until age six, all French three-year-olds are guaranteed a place in preschool, and over 95 percent of French children aged three to five attend. Similarly, Sweden's Educare, often cited internationally as the gold standard in early learning, provides subsidized childcare and education for the children of all working parents from the age of one through the start of formal schooling. In Finland, all families are entitled to childcare for their preschool-aged children. Japan and Germany also subsidize childcare, although both countries, like the United States, have insufficient placements for all families that need childcare.

During World War II, the United States looked as if it was on track to provide universal, government-subsidized childcare. The Lanham Act, in place from 1943 to 1946, is widely considered to be a milestone in the history of US childcare policy, primarily because it was the first, and only, federal program to serve children regardless of family income. As noted in Chapter 2, it was motivated by the need for women to work to aid the war effort. Commensurate with the times, the program ended as the war effort wound down and women were expected to return to the home.

Currently, the US federal government offers a patchwork of childcare assistance programs. Some are educational programs aimed at low-income families (e.g., Head Start), and others are subsidies that individuals can claim when they file their taxes. Currently, forty-three states provide publicly funded preschool programs with varying eligibility based on family income. Estimates also suggest that about 7 percent of US employers provide on-site childcare.

Difficulties that parents experience with childcare are costly. Studies show that nearly half of workers, mostly women, miss an average of four days of work annually because of childcare problems; this is estimated to cost businesses $4.4 billion a year in lost productivity and working families nearly $8.3 billion in lost wages.

How does childcare assistance affect a mother's ability to work?

Parents make choices about how best to combine work and family, but let's be clear: many parents don't have good choices. For example, about 25 percent of US families are headed by women, and current rules require that low-income women eligible for welfare cannot receive those benefits unless they are working or in some sort of education or training program. Hence, being a non-working parent is not even a choice for low-income women anymore. The government has chosen for them, and it is squarely on the side of work. For other women, a lack of access to affordable childcare can push parents (particularly mothers) out of the labor force, hindering their career growth and hence their long-term earnings potential.

Empirical research confirms that, particularly for lower-income families, childcare subsidies increase women's labor force participation. What we do not have much information about yet is whether firms that offer on-site or subsidized childcare experience better worker retention. If it turns out that they do, assisting employees with childcare could lead to greater wage growth for women and facilitate deeper loyalty to employers.

In an advanced economy such as the United States, the conversation about subsidized childcare should consider broad, long-term societal issues. Nobel laureate in economics James Heckman, for example, has become an outspoken advocate for government investment in early childhood education. He argues that while such education benefits mothers (and fathers) and their ability to work, it also has important, positive effects on children's developmental outcomes. He provides evidence that the impact of early childhood education on children's development and cognitive abilities will have far-reaching economic effects, including reducing the deficit, strengthening the economy, and reducing dependency on social welfare programs. He emphasizes that early childhood investments are a critical solution for ensuring that the United States maintains a skilled workforce.

4

HOW DO MEN AND WOMEN INTERACT IN THE WORKPLACE?

Women have made great strides in recent years in climbing the proverbial corporate ladder, yet obstacles still stand in the way of gender equity. Against this backdrop, we explore interactions between men and women in the workplace, the ways in which men's and women's interpersonal communication styles and behaviors are valued, and how these affect outcomes on the job. We also focus on how women's professional interactions and behaviors and the presence of female role models and leaders contribute to women's success.

Have women made inroads in business leadership?

Women make up 50 percent of the world's population and around 40 percent of its labor market participants, but they are woefully underrepresented among business leaders. Yet at the beginning of 2020, before the COVID-19 pandemic began, the representation of women holding leadership positions in corporate America was slowly increasing. Between 2015 and 2020, the share of women in senior vice president roles grew from 23 to 28 percent, and in the C-suite the share of women increased from 17 to 21 percent. As shown in Figure 4.1, women constituted 7.4 percent of CEOs of Fortune 500 companies in 2020; there were none in 1995.

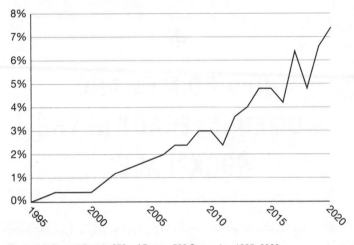

Figure 4.1 Percent Female CEOs of Fortune 500 Companies, 1995–2020
Source: Catalyst, Historical List of Women CEOs of the Fortune Lists.

This inability to get to the top is often referred to as the glass ceiling—the invisible barrier that keeps women from the top corporate jobs. *The Economist* magazine maintains an annual Glass-Ceiling Index, ranking twenty-nine countries on ten indicators of equality for women in the workplace, including educational attainment, labor force participation, earnings, childcare expenses, maternity and paternity rights, business school applications, and representation in senior jobs (management positions, company boards, and government). Iceland, Norway, and Sweden top the rankings, while the United States consistently falls below the average.

Leaders have enormous input into the culture of their firms and the hiring and promotion of those who work for them. If leaders are mostly men, and if they prefer to hire men, this can perpetuate the cycle of female disadvantage. The underrepresentation of women in lucrative leadership positions may help explain the persistence of the gender wage gap. And although women have made inroads into the top business jobs, the recession induced by the COVID-19 pandemic and its disproportionate burden on women threaten that progress.

Why are women underrepresented in the top business echelons?

In the United States, a vast majority, 93 percent, of the general public does not see major differences between men and women on key business leadership qualities, as shown by a Pew Research survey of US adults. Despite this confidence, women remain underrepresented in the highest-paying positions in the business world. Why might this be the case? Almost half of those surveyed felt that women were held to higher standards of performance than men and that this hindered their progress.[1]

The recent gains for women in corporate leadership are part of a broader set of changes in women's economic lives that started around the 1970s. In addition to the remarkable rise in women's LFPR (particularly of married women with children), women's education and entry into business management positions have also increased. Figure 4.2 shows the percent of women and men aged twenty-five to thirty-four who are college graduates from 1940 to 2018. For decades women lagged behind men in terms of education, but by the mid-1990s women earned the majority of college degrees. And by the early 2000s, women earned nearly half of professional degrees, as shown in Figure 4.3.

These gains in LFPR, college education, and professional degrees will likely translate into more women leaders, but this process takes time. As more women gain experience and move through the leadership pipeline, this should be reflected in their representation in the upper ranks of the corporate hierarchy. This pipeline hypothesis predicts continued gains for women in leadership. Yet the gains at the very top have been discouragingly slow. What might explain that?

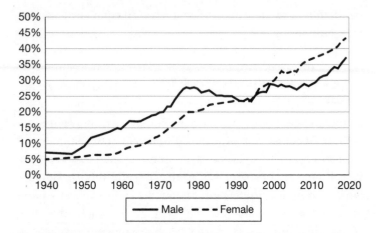

Figure 4.2 Percent College Graduates Among Men and Women Aged 25–34, 1940–2019
Source: US Census Bureau.

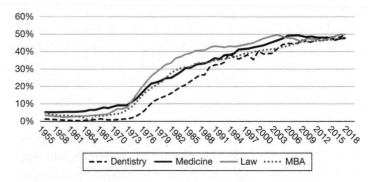

Figure 4.3 Percent Female Graduates in Selected Professional Programs, 1995–2018
Source: Digest of Education Statistics.

For one thing, the pipeline is notoriously leaky in that women (more so than men) disappear on their way to the top. Some women decide that corporate leadership positions, with their attendant long hours and notoriously inflexible schedules, are simply not compatible with family responsibilities. Complicating the issue, the lack of female role models and mentoring likely discourages other women from attaining positions at the top of the corporate hierarchy. Furthermore, numerous studies find that women are more risk-averse than men. A willingness to take risks helps employees compete for higher-paying jobs and negotiate higher salaries. Women may take themselves out of the running for top jobs because they are less interested in working in a highly competitive corporate environment.

The leaky pipeline cannot fully explain why so few women are at the top. Even women who want to climb the ladder to the C-suite encounter roadblocks. One of these roadblocks is sex discrimination, which likely increases as one moves up the corporate hierarchy. This can occur when men dislike sharing power and prestige with women or believe women to be less capable. Discrimination is particularly acute for Black women, who are likely to experience discrimination on the basis both of gender and race.

In addition, when women leaders act in ways that are consistent with gender stereotypes (e.g., focusing on building relationships or expressing concerns for other people's perspectives), they are often viewed as less competent leaders. Yet if women act in ways that are inconsistent with such stereotypes (acting assertively, displaying ambition), their behavior can be judged as unfeminine, which can also hinder their ascent to the top. Sometimes the discrimination is less overt. Equally qualified women may, for example, not be offered opportunities for promotion and advancement if their (male) supervisors are concerned that they may leave the workforce to have children. Women are often stereotyped, their career commitments treated the same whether they plan to have children or not.

Despite increasing investment in their own careers, women are not yet calling the shots in the corporate world. This underrepresentation not only deprives women of higher earnings but also deprives society as a whole of their perspectives, considerable talents, and potential contributions to the economy.

Are there differences in how women and men network and does it matter for career success?

Networking is an activity often dreaded by men and women alike. Mingling in rooms full of people or approaching senior colleagues to ask for advice can be intimidating. It is clearly perceived as beneficial; college career centers regularly sponsor networking events to help students find jobs, and self-help books are filled with advice for would-be networkers.

Plenty of anecdotal evidence suggests that networking is important and that men are somehow better at it. Social scientists have noted that there are two types of networks: instrumental networks, with a professional focus on work-related advice and information, and friendship networks, which fulfill a social function. Particularly in male-dominated industries, it is easier for men to connect in both social and instrumental networks with other men who have been through (or in fact may control) evaluation and promotion. Therefore, their instrumental and friendship networks may substantially overlap and result in deeper relationships in both spheres. Women, on the other hand, typically form friendship networks with other women, but because they are less represented in managerial positions, they may have to form instrumental networks that consist mainly of men. Women's weaker friendship ties within their instrumental network may leave them without the same flow of information and advocacy at the upper levels as their male colleagues.

Data on professional networking are scarce, so economists turn to experiments to understand the benefits of networks. An experiment is ideal because observing real networking and drawing conclusions is tricky. For example, if a woman does not join colleagues after work for drinks, is it because she does not wish to network or because she faces childcare constraints? And if she did join her colleagues for a drink, would that further her career—in other words, would her networking even matter? The experiments on networking are designed to understand differences in the use and impact of networks, when both women and men have the same opportunities.

In one experiment participants are divided into groups and complete three stages of an experiment: the task, networking, and allocation stages.[2] They repeat the experiment several times to mimic the real-life experience of having repeated interactions with colleagues. The three stages represent work environments, where work is produced and then networking is used to achieve pay increases or promotion. The results indicated that men and women have similar tendencies to network when given the opportunity. However, gender pay and promotion gaps arose, because men are more likely to network with other men and favor their network members when distributing pay. The results of this experiment suggest that as long as men remain in positions of power, networking disadvantages women. Of course, equal opportunities to network are less likely in the real business world since women take on the majority of caregiving, limiting their time outside of work for such activities and thus reducing their access to career advancement.

Does working for a female manager enhance women's careers?

One might imagine that women benefit from having a female boss. Female bosses, knowing what women experience in the business world, may organize work in a way that is less gender-biased and more family-friendly. However, it is actually quite complicated to ascertain the impact of a manager's gender on career success, because, for example, managers may be assigned based on the performance of their subordinates. To address such concerns, managers would have to be randomly assigned. One study addressed this concern by leveraging the practice of a large firm that rotated its assignment of managers so that the gender of the manager was essentially random for a particular employee.[3]

What they found was not surprising. Male employees transitioning from a female manager to a male manager were promoted more quickly than those male employees who transitioned from a male manager to a female manager. Female employees experienced similar promotion rates regardless of the gender of their manager. In short, the study showed that the size of this male-to-male promotion advantage explains over one-third of the gender gap in pay grades at this firm.

The promotion advantage for men occurred in situations where the male manager and employee worked in close physical proximity, which suggests that social interactions may explain this advantage. In fact, a survey of employees at this firm confirmed this hypothesis. Male employees were more likely to spend breaks with their managers after switching from a female manager to a male manager. This proximity led to sharing of information, such as a favorite sports team, and strengthened their social ties. Female employees, on the other hand, experienced no change in the amount of time spent with managers after such a switch. Of course, these data are from one firm and focused on an office environment, so it is hard to know if the results are generalizable to other settings. Other studies, also focused on professional workers, have found that when the share of women in a higher rank increases, the gender gap in promotions from the lower rank is significantly reduced. A study inclusive of a wider range of workers (e.g., skilled and less-skilled) tracks employees displaced by plant closings. Comparing men and women displaced from the same plant closing and hired into the same new plant, they find that women face larger wage reductions, but this penalty is smaller for those women hired into firms with female leadership. Taken together, these findings indicate that increasing the number of female managers would help level the playing field for women.

Do women need mentors and does it matter who they are?

Lack of access to informal mentoring and networking opportunities has long been assumed to be a disadvantage for women. A mentor is a seasoned colleague who helps guide the career of a less-experienced co-worker by imparting knowledge, expertise, and wisdom. Women are often said to be particularly in need of mentors to help them break through the glass ceiling. Research on mentoring is abundant. The evidence from a wide array of scholarly disciplines points to benefits for women from participating in mentoring programs. Many of these studies compare women who sought out mentoring to those who did not and found that those who participated were more successful in their careers. But what does that tell us? That women who seek out mentoring are perhaps more highly motivated and would have advanced anyway? We need to look further to confirm the benefits of mentoring for women.

To know whether a random employee would benefit from mentoring, we turn to our own profession, economics. The Committee on the Status of Women in the Economics Profession (CSWEP) has long maintained data on the number of women in economics in higher education, from undergraduates through faculty. The percentage of undergraduate female economics majors has been remarkably steady for decades, at about 35 percent. For those women who go on to study economics at the doctoral level and enter academic careers, the prospects are disheartening. In doctorate-granting institutions, while about 30 percent of newly hired economics faculty are women, only about 5 percent of full professors are women. This drop-off from entry-level jobs to more senior-level jobs indicates in part what we have referred to as a "leaky pipeline."

In response to these dismal numbers, CSWEP started a two-day intensive mentoring program for new faculty members where mentees obtained advice on publishing, teaching, and balancing work and family responsibilities from senior female faculty. The workshop occurs annually but slots are limited. Every year a random group of applicants is invited to attend.[4] The surplus of applicants coupled with the random invitation procedure creates treatment and control groups, as in a randomized controlled trial. Follow-up interviews with both participants and non-participants occur between four and fourteen years later. Responses indicated that the workshops helped female economists who attended build lasting relationships with peers and mentors, remain in academe, and gain tenure in selective departments compared to their peers who were not able to participate. This relatively simply mentoring intervention helped female economists achieve academic career success.

In the male-dominated fields of science, technology, engineering, and mathematics (STEM), female advisors and professors have been found to be important for the success of female students. STEM fields, which typically require highly analytical training, offer high wages and career advancement for women. Federal scientific research agencies, policymakers, and educators have placed a priority on advancing representation of women in these fields.

How does having female representation on boards of directors help women?

Serving on the board of directors (BOD) of a company provides the ability to make key personnel decisions and set a tone for the company that might benefit women down the ladder. Yet all too often BODs are composed primarily of white men. Can making BODs more gender-equal enhance the careers of the women at the companies they oversee? We might expect corporate boards to exert the most influence on the appointment of C-suite employees as opposed to the rank-and-file workforce because boards are generally responsible for appointing (and firing) the CEO of the company.

Several countries believe BODs can have an important impact on gender equality. In 2003, Norway was the first country to pass a law requiring a minimum of 40 percent of each gender on the BODs of most companies. The law took effect in 2005, and by 2008 all firms had complied. Since that time, Austria, Belgium, Denmark, France, Ireland, Iceland, Italy, Germany, the Netherlands, and Spain have adopted similar regulations. The United States has not formally adopted quotas, but since

2009, companies taking action on electing board members must publicly report the results. Even this non-binding action may encourage board diversity, perhaps because companies fear the imposition of quotas or because it shifts norms about diversity.

The implementation of these quotas has unequivocally increased the number of women on BODs. In the European Union, female board representation increased from 12 percent in 2010 to 23 percent in 2019. In contrast, in the United States the number was 18 percent in 2018. At the same time, Japan reports only 5 percent. Clearly, quotas are effective in improving gender representation on BODs.

The advent of the quota laws provided an opportunity to study the impact of female board membership because these laws caused a nearly random change to the gender composition of boards. Prior to this, companies with relatively high percentages of women on BODs were not representative because they were likely to be those with more progressive views around many issues of management, making it difficult to ascertain the effect of women directors on various outcomes. For example, do these BOD laws help further the careers of the women who work at the firms or equalize the pay of men and women? Using Norwegian data, one study found that quota implementation had little discernible impact on women in business beyond its direct effect on the women who made it into boardrooms, who experienced higher earnings as a result.[5] Researchers focusing on Italy, which has one of the lowest female LFPRs among developed countries, came to a similar conclusion—the strict enforcement of gender quotas did not improve the gender wage gap or the hiring of women.[6] However, Italy's quota, in place only for a three-year period, may not have allowed enough time for positive effects of increased female representation to take root. Newly appointed board members may not wield enough power to affect long-entrenched gender norms. It is disheartening to find that in

Norway and Italy, although gender representation on BODs increased, there was no effect on women lower down the corporate ladder.

Why aren't women always heard in the workplace?

There is no doubt that men and women approach many things differently in the workplace; communication style is no exception. Women tend to modify their statements with questions, use more noticeably polite language, and refer to experiences and emotions more frequently than men. Women often speak to establish connections, while men exhibit communication behaviors that establish authority and status.

Gender communication differences are so pronounced that a new vocabulary is emerging that names gender-specific communication behaviors. "Mansplaining" (a man explaining something to a woman in a condescending way that assumes she has no knowledge about the topic) "bropropriating" or "bro-opting" (when a man takes credit for a woman's idea), and "manterruption" (an unnecessary interruption of a woman by a man) have made their way into common vernacular. The phenomenon of manterruption was painfully demonstrated when Kanye West grabbed the microphone from nineteen-year-old award-winner Taylor Swift at the 2009 Video Music Awards to give his opinion of the injustice of her award. More recently, during the vice presidential debate in 2020, then-candidate Kamala Harris had to assert herself in the face of interruptions from Mike Pence with "Mr. Vice President, I'm speaking."

Patterns of women experiencing more frequent interruptions are well documented by researchers; a number of recent studies highlight such behaviors in professional settings at all levels. It has been shown to happen in the classroom, in casual conversation, during doctor visits with female physicians, and in the workplace. In male-dominated academic fields like economics and engineering, more frequent and time-consuming interruptions and questions to female speakers are common occurrences. That these often happen during presentations as part of a job interview means the stakes are high.

Women speaking at US congressional hearings, both as members of Congress and as invited speakers, are more likely to be interrupted than men.[7] Perhaps most surprising is the interruption of women at one of the highest professional levels, the US Supreme Court. A study found that interruptions of female justices by males have increased since the 1990s, and by 2015 women justices were both less likely to interrupt anyone (33 percent less likely) and far more likely to be the targets of interruption (a whopping 300 percent more often).[8] Most surprising is that 10 percent of the interruptions of female justices came from male advocates arguing cases before the court, and not their male judicial colleagues; this despite the fact that Court rules dictate that advocates stop speaking when one of the justices begins to speak. Female justices were more likely to use "female" communication patterns, including more polite language, but these polite tendencies diminished with time on the Court, perhaps to deter interruptions.

Researchers have noted that men disproportionately dominate professional conversations, and only when women make up a majority of a meeting's participants are women and men heard equally. Of course, women could use "male" communication styles, but the result is not the same. Interruption and taking credit are viewed quite differently when the speaker is a woman; men who dominate a conversation are viewed as decisive and strong leaders, while such behaviors by women are often viewed as pushy and rude. In a research study, professional men and women were shown resumes of a fictional CEO, with the name at the top, either Jennifer or John, indicating gender. Their applications included information, manipulated randomly by the researcher, indicating that the applicant tended to speak either more or less than others in their position. Despite having the same qualifications, John received 10 percent higher marks than his peers for speaking more during meetings, while Jennifer was penalized 14 percent compared to her peers for similar behavior.[9] Given the boost to men when women remain silent and the cost to women of speaking out, professional women find themselves in a no-win situation.

Silencing women comes at a cost, both to women and to employers. Good ideas that can boost the performance of a firm are lost or ignored, although the magnitude of this loss is difficult to quantify. Progress in diversity and the positive changes that result from female managers and women in leadership are also sacrificed when women's voices are silenced or ignored.

Is there a gender gap in self-promotion? Does it matter?

Self-promotion of one's accomplishments and strengths can play an important role in educational and career success. Unfortunately, women often feel uncomfortable advertising their accomplishments. It may be that women downplay their own contributions to avoid cognitive dissonance with their communal (team) approach, clashes with society's view of gender roles, or backlash that results from negative views of women who are vocal in self-promoting. Of course, self-promotion is considered appropriate to men's roles and thus more often carries positive connotations rather than social backlash for men.

Within our world of academic research, men describe their work differently than do women. For example, life science and medical research articles with a senior male author are much more likely to include laudatory terms like "novel" and "unprecedented" to describe the research.[10] Drawing attention to the importance of their work in this way leads to different perceptions of their work, increasing the likelihood that their work is considered influential and cited. Ultimately these perceptions can positively affect the probability of promotion and higher salary for these researchers.

It is complicated to know if women are systematically underpromoting equal achievements relative to men. First one must know what their achievements are, and then one must compare the way they communicate them. Lack of data on these components has resulted in a dearth of research. An experimental research approach helps solve this problem.[11] The setup is pretty simple: male and female research subjects take a well-known standardized test, the Armed Services Vocational Aptitude Battery, are informed of their scores, and then asked to provide an evaluation of their performance. They were asked to indicate their agreement (from 1 to 100) with statements such as "I performed well on the test" and then to rate their overall performance ranging from "terrible" to "exceptional." The subjective nature of these questions is purposeful—if participants were simply asked to report their scores, they would be making a decision about lying, not self-promotion.[12] Patterns in the responses indicated that women, compared to equally performing men, evaluated themselves 33 percent less favorably. This sizable gap narrows only slightly when all research subjects are fully informed of their own score and their relative achievement within the group. A similar result was found in a related experiment: equally qualified men rated themselves 33 percent higher than comparable women—and were more frequently hired as a result.[13]

Because the reluctance of women to self-promote may have its roots both in inherent personality traits and in ingrained social norms adopted by women, acting differently always carries the possibility of social backlash, including negative consequences to their careers. Women in a professional development program reported that "being less visible in the office could hurt their odds of promotion. But they worried that violating feminine norms could leave them even worse off."[14] Except for in a few limited contexts (ironically, working in a male-dominated occupation is one), women who adopt masculine self-promotion strategies are perceived negatively. The combination of gender-role-compatible styles being ineffective and masculine styles engendering backlash against women leaves no clear path to success. Institutional change, including recognition of the value of "communal" skills, may be necessary to even the playing field.

How does sexual harassment (and the #MeToo Movement) affect women in the workplace?

Title VII of the Civil Rights Act of 1964 is the cornerstone of anti-discrimination law in the United States. It prohibits employment discrimination on the basis of race, color, religion, sex, or national origin. Over time, this law has been interpreted to cover sexual harassment as a form of discrimination. The Equal Employment Opportunity Commission (EEOC) is charged with upholding this law.

Sexual harassment can be defined in two ways. Perhaps the more obvious is quid pro quo, where employees are expected to provide sexual favors in exchange for employment opportunities such as raises or promotions. However, the law also protects workers against a hostile work environment whereby employees are subjected to sexually charged language and/or gestures. Under the hostile environment scenario, the sexual harassment must be so severe or pervasive as to negatively impact the employee's working conditions.

Three-quarters of people who experience workplace harassment fail to report it, often out of fear of retaliation. Another possible reason for underreporting is that employees who are subjected to inappropriate behavior aren't clear on when it crosses the line into illegal harassment.

The #MeToo movement, a social movement launched in the fall of 2017 by sexual harassment survivor and activist Tarana Burke, has heightened awareness of this issue. #MeToo has gone viral and helped to expose reprehensible behavior by (mostly) men at the top of their industries. Film producer Harvey Weinstein is one of the highest-profile sexual harassers, due to the media attention that he and many of his victims command. Many companies responded to the attention surrounding #MeToo with policy changes such as mandatory training on the subject and new guidelines for reporting and handling sexual harassment. Unfortunately, some of these efforts seem to have elicited unexpected and unfortunate outcomes. In one survey, 19 percent of male respondents said they were reluctant to hire attractive women, and 21 percent said they were reluctant to hire women for jobs involving close interpersonal interactions with men.[15]

Figure 4.4 shows the prevalence of sexual harassment over time and illustrates that after a decline, filings rose sharply after the fall of 2017. It is difficult, however, to attribute this increase in filings exclusively to #MeToo, since other factors were in play. Although the vast majority of cases are filed by women, nearly one-fifth are filed by men. Harassment claims are filed in a wide variety of industries, but particularly high rates prevail in the restaurant and agricultural industries, which employ a high number of less-educated women.

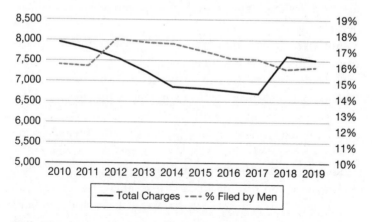

Figure 4.4 Total Sexual Harassment Charges Filed with the EEOC and Percent Filed by Men, 2010–2019

Source: EEOC.

Is sexual harassment detrimental to a firm's value? If so, more proactive approaches to weeding out harassers may be needed. In a preliminary study, researchers searched the on-line job sites Indeed and Glassdoor for comments related to sexual harassment and calculated the percentage of company reviews in which these comments appeared.[16] Comparing stock returns for firms with differing reports of sexual harassment while taking into account other factors that affect stock prices revealed that more harassment comments were associated with lower stock prices.

Firms may pay a price in other ways. Employees who are sexually harassed may be less productive if victims are unable to focus on their jobs due to worries about harassment or decide not to put forth their maximum effort as a response to the negative work environment. Comparing the performance of mutual funds managed by females and males both before and after the Weinstein scandal, one study found that funds managed by women had improved their performance after the scandal and male-managed funds fell in value, even when other factors affecting fund performance were taken into consideration.[17] The threat of harassment for victims and fear of punishment for perpetrators appeared to alter worker performance.

Anti-harassment training is now widespread in US corporations, but its effectiveness is questionable.[18] Could female leadership reduce the incidence of sexual harassment? Perhaps a female boss will not put up with (mostly) men harassing women at the workplace. Indeed, she may be more attuned to harassment. In fact, studies show that female leadership is correlated with lower levels of sexual harassment.[19]

Research indicates that sexual harassment harms worker productivity and firm profits and that female leadership has the potential to reduce such harassment. A study linking sexual harassment claims within industries to individual-level earnings data found that in industries where sexual harassment is more common, women receive higher wages. This compensating differential—a wage boost that exists net of other wage-enhancing factors—is essentially a pay increase for facing a greater risk of sexual harassment.[20]

5

WHAT LEADS TO THE GENDER PAY GAP?

In this chapter we revisit the issue of gender differences in earnings. From 1960 to 1980, women earned approximately 60 percent of what men earned. This ratio started to rise in the 1970s, the rise gained traction in the 1980s, and by the mid-2000s the gap had narrowed such that women earned about 81 percent of what men earned. While the difference between men's and women's pay is well known, few understand its evolution, and its underlying causes are heavily debated. Here we explain how a pay ratio is calculated, show its evolution, and help readers disentangle factors that might be considered legitimate sources of pay differences from those that might reflect gender pay discrimination. Many factors determine individual wages. In this chapter we try to understand the contributions of various factors to the evolving gender pay gap. If we hope to close it, then we must understand the relative importance (and causes) of these factors.

How are wages determined?

Because the subject of this chapter and Chapters 6 and 7 is women's (and men's) earnings, a basic understanding of how earnings are determined is necessary. It turns out that economists are quite precise in their use of the terms "earnings," "wages," and "salaries." We think of people paid on an hourly basis as earning an hourly wage, and multiplying that wage by their hours of work gives us their earnings. In contrast, many workers are paid an annual salary. And if we know the total number of hours they work per year, we can calculate their approximate hourly wage.

To explain why people's earnings differ, economists rely on a model of the labor market. The concept of supply and demand is central to economics and comparatively easy to understand. Each of us is a potential supplier of our own labor; think of this supply as measured by the number of hours we are willing to work at various wage rates. The key to this decision for an individual is whether the wage offered by an employer is of greater value to them than the value of their time outside of the market. In other words, is it worth it to the individual to give up leisure time or time that could be used in home production in favor of that time in the labor force? It seems logical that the higher the wage rate, the more hours people are willing to work. This is the (upward-sloping) supply curve for labor in a nutshell.

On the other side of the market, firms hire workers in order to get things done. The value of a worker to a firm is the additional output that worker can produce and, in general terms, is referred to as productivity. A firm is willing to hire a worker as long as the value of her productivity exceeds the wage that the firm must pay. This is where individual wages will differ, because particular workers have higher or lower productivity levels. The higher the wages for a given level of productivity, the more costly labor is to firms; they will look for alternatives and perhaps cut back on production. So as wages go up, the number of workers hired tends to fall—represented by a (downward-sloping) demand curve.

The combination of these two groups, workers and firms, suppliers and demanders, is what ultimately determines wages. When represented graphically, the intersection of the supply and demand curves determines what economists call the equilibrium wage. Suppose that the equilibrium wage is $25 per hour for a particular type of labor. Firms know that they don't need to pay more than this amount to attract employees; doing so would increase costs. Likewise, firms offering less than the equilibrium wage will find that they cannot hire enough workers unless they raise wages until the equilibrium wage is reached.

What does the equilibrium wage tell us? It is a representation of the average wage within a labor market. Of course, there are markets for many different types of labor. No one expects an accountant to earn the same as a recent high school graduate. Because of occupation and industry differences in profitability and differences in workers' productivity levels, individuals' wages will vary from a single equilibrium wage.

There are a number of characteristics that determine productivity. Many are easy to observe, like a worker's occupation and industry, individual characteristics such as education and work experience, and hours of work. Other characteristics and behaviors that affect productivity are less easy to observe but nevertheless are likely to be reflected in earnings. These largely unobservable factors include intellectual ability (often correlated with higher education), motivation to work hard, biological differences that may lead to differences in decision-making, physical strength, and absenteeism, among others.

In addition to the determinants of productivity, wages can differ simply as part of the process used to set the wage for each individual worker. Because the equilibrium wage rate is an average, an individual's wage is often established by an interaction between the employer and employee during the hiring process. The exact process varies by occupation and industry but often involves negotiation. As a consequence, gender differences in competitiveness, risk-taking, and willingness to negotiate aggressively can result in different salaries.

What is not formally addressed in this analysis is labor market discrimination. After accounting for "legitimate" productivity differences, remaining gender pay differences may reflect discrimination. Pay discrimination can occur for a variety of reasons; more detailed explanations are covered in Chapter 6. Suffice it to say that discrimination is difficult to measure because one also needs to measure individual productivity—more on that in a minute.

It is worth noting that the equilibrium wage is driven by market forces. Markets are valued for gathering information and providing incentives for efficient outcomes, but they do not ensure a just, fair, or living wage. Society may determine that the prevailing market wage is too low for some groups and impose a federal minimum wage, as the United States did beginning in 1932. Individual states and even municipalities have the ability to mandate minimum wages higher than the federal minimum, but not lower. There are other ways in which wages are regulated; labor unions, for example, play a role in setting the wages for their members through a collective bargaining process with the employer. And many public employers (along with some private employers) impose wage structures in order to improve equality.

How do we measure the gender pay gap?

Most surveys that ask about income collect data on earnings and hours of work, which allows researchers to calculate an hourly wage, even for those paid an annual salary. When we make comparisons, we generally use men's and women's median annual earnings for those working full-time and year-round. This eliminates inconsistencies inherent in comparing people who work substantially different numbers of hours. The median is used because the average is sensitive to outliers (for example, including Jeff Bezos's earnings would make the mean wage appear much higher). And because women are far more likely than men to work part-time or part of the year, it does not make sense to compare the earnings of all men and women; a more accurate comparison is between men and women who work full-time year-round.

There are two ways to compare men's and women's earnings that are pretty standard. One is called the gender wage gap. This is simply [(median male earnings – median female earnings)/median male earnings] × 100. If men earned $100 per hour and women earned $80 an hour, the gap would be 20 percent. However, the more common way to compare men's and women's earnings is to look at the ratio of men's earnings to women's earnings (and sometimes express that as a percentage). In our example, this would be 80/100 for a wage ratio of 0.80, so we would say that women earned 80 percent of what men earned. You can see that these are just two sides of the same coin. Because the gap and the ratio provide the same information, we use both terms in what follows.

How big is the gender pay gap? Does it vary for women of color? For immigrants? By sexual orientation?

Federal agencies such as the US Census Bureau, Department of Education, and Bureau of Labor Statistics conduct surveys of individuals, households, and businesses to gather information about people's earnings. Unless otherwise stated, for all calculations in this chapter we use data from the 2019 ACS for year-round, full-time workers aged sixteen and over. In some cases we narrow our age range to the prime working age, which is twenty-five to sixty-four years. These are people who have largely finished their education and are not yet retired. While the CPS may be preferable for earnings, it lacks sufficient sample size for examining smaller demographic groups. As of 2019, data from the ACS indicate that the ratio of women's to men's median earnings for those aged sixteen and over working year-round and full-time was 80 percent, with women's median earnings at $43,436 and men's at $53,538. Perhaps in recognition of this persistent inequality, the makers of the board game Monopoly have come out with a version called Ms. Monopoly, which favors women—they earn more, for example, when they pass Go.

Geography plays a role as well, as shown in Figure 5.1. The gender pay ratio ranges from a high of 92 percent in Hawaii to a low of 66 percent in Wyoming. Why so much variation? While pinning down a single reason is not possible, one explanation is the composition of industries in each state. Consider the states with the lowest pay ratios, Wyoming and Utah, with ratios of 66 percent, and 71 percent, respectively. Slightly more than 29 percent of the employment in Wyoming and 26 percent in Utah is in three industries: agriculture/forestry/fishing/hunting/mining, construction, and wholesale trade. The national average of employment in these industries is just 23 percent. These are all male-dominated industries with high rates of union representation and that pay relatively high salaries. On the other end of the scale, Hawaii, Maryland, and New York, with pay ratios of 92, 89, and 87 percent, respectively, have less than 15 percent of employment in these three male-dominated industries. Instead, employment is skewed toward industries in which women are more included, and

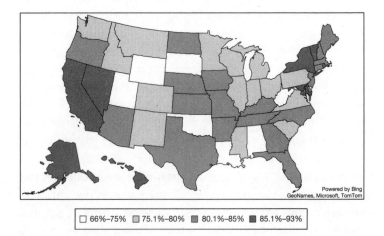

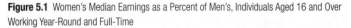

Figure 5.1 Women's Median Earnings as a Percent of Men's, Individuals Aged 16 and Over Working Year-Round and Full-Time

Source: 2019 ACS.

pay is more equal across genders. In Maryland, for example, employment in public administration is nearly three times the national average. Given the importance of tourism in Hawaii, it is not surprising that 14 percent of employment is in the arts/entertainment/recreation/accommodation/food service industry. This is more than double the national average of 7 percent. This industry is known to pay more equal salaries to men and women. The pattern of employment in Hawaii is also notable for the high proportion of people employed in the military: 9 percent, compared to 1 percent nationally. As we will see, earnings for women and men are closest in the military.

We caution that the gender pay ratio does not tell the full story. While Connecticut has a pay ratio of 82 percent, women there have median earnings of $55,558, whereas in Vermont, where the gender pay ratio is 92 percent, women's median earnings are lower at $47,477. Other factors that can affect the pay ratio across states include minimum wages and the extent of labor union membership.

In addition to geographic differences, pay ratios vary substantially by race and ethnicity. In Table 5.1, we show women's earnings as a percent of men's for all women, and disaggregated into racial and ethnic groups. Because non-Hispanic white men have historically enjoyed positions of power and privilege in the economy, we show gender ratios both within race

Table 5.1 Ratio of Median Earnings of Women to Men for Year-Round, Full-Time Workers Aged 16 and Over by Race/Ethnicity

	Women	Men	Within-Race Earnings Ratio	Earnings Ratio (Compared to White Men)
White	$48,487	$60,609	80%	80%
Black	$37,981	$40,406	94%	63%
Hispanic	$33,335	$40,406	83%	55%
Asian	$55,558	$70,710	79%	92%

Source: 2019 ACS.

and compared to non-Hispanic white men. The numbers are striking. Hispanic women earn only 55 percent of what white men earn, while Black women do a little better at 63 percent. Asian women have the most favorable ratio compared to white men, at 92 percent, and white women earn 80 percent of what white men earn. Black and Hispanic women fare better when the comparison is within race/ethnicity. This is because Black and Hispanic men have much lower earnings compared to non-Hispanic white men.

It is more difficult to measure gender wage gaps by sexual orientation due to a lack of data. Starting in 2013, the ACS asked respondents in partnerships to identify whether their partner is of the same sex. Thus, we can obtain very good wage information from this survey for partnered lesbians. It is not possible to tell a respondent's sexual orientation in the ACS if they are single. The 2019 ACS data indicate that the ratio of median earnings of partnered lesbians to those of white men is 87 percent. To calculate a pay ratio for single lesbians, we then turned to the Behavioral Risk Factor Surveillance System (BRFSS) data—from a large telephone survey that the Centers for Disease Control administers annually. Calculations from the BRFSS data over the years 2014–2019, for states that opted to include the sexual orientation module, indicate that single lesbians earned median income equal to 73 percent of single white males' income.[1] This difference in earnings ratios for lesbians by marital status is in keeping with studies that show that partnered lesbians tend to earn more than their single counterparts.

Finally, immigrant women earn 85 percent of what immigrant men earn. This is in contrast to US-born women, who earn 80 percent of what US-born men earn. In the United States, immigrants are a heterogeneous group. Some immigrants arrive to fill skilled jobs, while others have low skills. Table 5.2 shows earnings for immigrants aged twenty-five to sixty-four by whether they have at least a college education.

Table 5.2 Median Earnings by Gender, Education and Nativity for Year-Round, Full-Time Workers Aged 25–64

	Women	Men	Within-Education and Nativity Earnings Ratio
Foreign-born and less than college	$30,304	$38,386	79%
Foreign-born and college or more	$68,690	$90,913	76%
US-born and less than college	$36,365	$49,497	73%
US-born and college or more	$62,629	$85,862	73%

Source: 2019 ACS.

Highly educated immigrant women earn 76 percent of what highly educated immigrant men earn, while at the lower education levels, immigrant women earn 79 percent of what their male immigrant counterparts earn. This compares to 73 percent for those who are US-born, regardless of their education.

Has the gap improved since the 1950s?

Figure 5.2 plots the gender wage ratio expressed as a percent from 1953 to 2019. In the 1950s and 1960s, the ratio hovered around 60 percent. It rose in the 1970s, but during the 1980s (the same decade that brought us widening income inequality) the gap between men's and women's earnings narrowed from 63 percent to 70 percent. More recently, it continues to rise, albeit quite a bit more slowly—from 2009 to 2019, the ratio rose by 5.7 percent. An analysis of early-release data by the Institute for Women's Policy Research noted an improvement in the gender pay ratio for women of all races between 2019 and 2020, a period that includes impacts from the COVID-19 pandemic. They attribute this not to true gains for women but to the exit of lower-paid women from the workforce due to pandemic-related job losses or the need

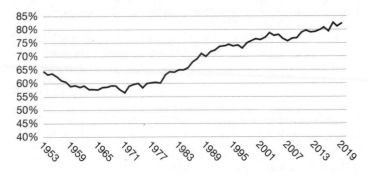

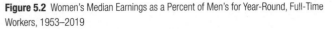

Figure 5.2 Women's Median Earnings as a Percent of Men's for Year-Round, Full-Time Workers, 1953–2019

Source: US Census Bureau.

to leave work to care for children, leaving the higher-paid in the sample.[2]

Although the pay ratio held steady near 60 percent through the 1970s, beneath the surface a great deal was changing in the labor force that warrants a more detailed look. Until the mid-1950s, the female labor force was composed primarily of single women and a smaller number of married women who worked more or less continuously (and rarely had families). These women actually had more education on average than working men at the time. Yet they earned only about 60 percent of what men earned. Part of this was that women (even those with college educations) were typically relegated to a narrow set of lower-paying occupations such as secretary, teacher, nurse, and librarian. And workplace discrimination was legal until 1963, so firms could, and often did, pay women less than men, even for doing the same job.

As more women began working for pay, the composition of women in the workforce began to change. Rather than being a select group of relatively well-educated women with few family responsibilities, a broader cross-section of women began to work, and the average education level of working women fell relative to working men. In addition, as women began

to cycle in and out of the labor force due to family responsibilities—rather than remaining always in or always out—a
substantial gender gap in years of labor market experience developed. These two factors helped keep the gender wage gap
relatively low between 1960 and 1979, a period during which
the ratio barely moves even though women were facing less
discrimination and making progress entering previously male-
dominated occupations. They were simply bringing fewer
skills to the workforce.

In the 1980s, the gender earnings ratio for year-round, full-
time workers increased substantially. What accounted for this
increase? Much of the wage gap closure in the 1980s had to do
with women's increasing education and, because women were
increasingly likely to work continuously, the narrowing of the
work experience gap with men. They also continued to enter
into previously male-dominated fields with higher wages, and
the rewards to their experience and education came closer to
those of men. What is interesting about the closing of the gap
during the 1980s is that the labor market itself was not favorable to women, particularly lower-skilled women. One research team that focused on the closure of the gender wage gap
in the 1980s described it as women "swimming upstream"—
changes in the labor market in the 1980s were working against
closing the gap, but declining discrimination and improvement in women's skills, coupled with declining earnings for
men, were enough to offset that.

By the time we reach the 2000s, the wage ratio reaches and
remains above 75 percent (albeit in some years just barely), and
the recognition that women and men earn different amounts—
even within the same occupation—moves to the forefront of
explanations for the gender pay gap. It is possible that women
find niches within even professional occupations that allow
them to meet both family and professional responsibilities,
and that these subfields often pay less. Within the field of law,
for example, women might work in the lower-paying trusts
and estates subfield while men work as higher-paid litigators.

Women physicians often gravitate toward family practice, with its more predictable hours and relatively lower pay, while men physicians may become surgeons, who are often required to be on call around the clock and are highly paid. Some jobs disproportionately reward long hours and total dedication (e.g., the finance industry) and offer the requisite high pay needed to attract employees. Others, such as pharmacy, take advantage of technology that allows for job sharing, an option typically more attractive to women than to men. Women's dual responsibilities as workers and caretakers of their families continue to limit their pay, even in the current era.

How does the pay gap vary across countries?

Figure 5.3 shows women's earnings as a percent of men's for selected countries from lowest to highest. There is considerable variation across countries, ranging from South Korea, where women earn only 68 cents for every dollar earned by men, to Belgium, with its very high ratio of 96 percent. In several countries women earn 90 percent or more of what men earn. The United States is on the lower end of this spectrum. While a full accounting of the reasons for these cross-country differences is

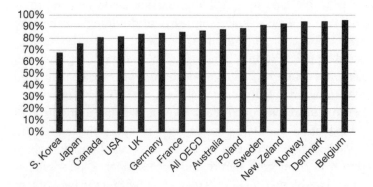

Figure 5.3 Women's Median Earnings as a Percent of Men's for Selected Countries
Source: OECD, 2019 or latest available.

beyond the scope of our text, differences in wage-setting policies, laws regarding equal pay, family-friendly policies, and expectations about the role of women in the economy all play important parts in explaining gender pay ratios.

What can we measure that might explain the reasons for gender pay differences?

Differences in education, work hours, experience, family responsibilities, occupation and industry, and union membership might justifiably explain gender pay differences. For each of these factors, there are two possible causes of pay differences.

First, women and men may simply have different levels of each of these factors (e.g., years of education or annual hours of work). If men have more education, for example, or work more hours, we would expect them to be paid more. No one expects a surgeon to make less than a barista (no matter how important that first cup of coffee is). Surgeons have invested more in their education and training; they are simply more productive. These differences are considered justifiable reasons for pay to vary.

Second, sometimes women and men are paid differently for the same level of each factor. Economists refer to this as the return on this factor. For example, this can occur when, all other factors being equal, a woman with a college degree is paid less than a man with the same college degree—a difference in returns to education based on gender. We close this section by describing and then using a statistical technique designed to examine how much of the gender pay gap is explained by differences in the amount of these justifiable factors versus how much is explained by gender differences in returns.

Can education level alone explain the gender pay gap?

We all know that wages are typically higher for workers with more education; that, after all, is the reason many people go to college. An investment in higher education hinges on the pay premium associated with a college degree. This premium is large and has remained large, even as there have been striking increases in the proportion of the population earning college degrees. But the question of whether the gender pay gap is caused by differences in educational attainment is complicated, and we will try to disentangle two different ways to think about the answer to this question.

The first way is to ask if the pay ratio favors men because they are more educated than women and therefore receive higher wages. This is an easy one. Although it was the case in the past, now the answer is a resounding no. In 2019, the average number of years of education for women between the ages of twenty-five and sixty-four was slightly higher than for men (13.8 years of education for women and 13.5 years for men). The proportion who had graduated from high school (91 percent of women and 88 percent of men) and who had earned a four-year college degree or more (37 percent of women compared to 32 percent of men) also highlights the educational advantage of women. It is only at the very highest levels of education—doctoral and professional degrees like those for professors (PhDs), physicians (MDs), and lawyers (JDs)—that men outperform women. Though 3.7 percent of men and 3.3 percent of women report doctoral and professional levels of education, these proportions are too small to account for the double-digit gender pay gap we have seen across the whole population. In fact, even this gender difference in doctoral degrees is already reversing, with women outpacing men in newly awarded doctoral degrees in 2018.[3]

The second way is to try to understand if men and women are paid the same when they have the same levels of education. Let's see what the pay gap looks like when we disaggregate by level of education, as shown in Figure 5.4. By dividing men and women into education groups, we can see that the pay ratio never approaches 100 percent—indicating that men

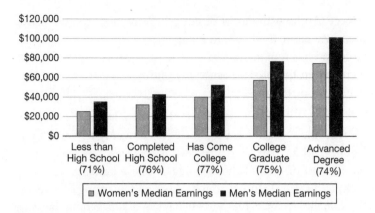

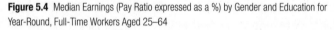

Figure 5.4 Median Earnings (Pay Ratio expressed as a %) by Gender and Education for Year-Round, Full-Time Workers Aged 25–64

Source: 2019 ACS.

and women with equal levels of education are not, in fact, paid equally. It is perhaps surprising that women with a high school education have a gender pay ratio (76 percent) that is slightly higher than those with an advanced degree (74 percent), as seen below the bars for each education category. Why would that be? If a large proportion of workers who have a high-school education are paid at or close to the minimum wage, this should result in a relatively high wage ratio. Among the well-educated, the levels of earnings highlight serious inequities. For example, women with an advanced degree actually have median earnings less than those of men with a four-year college degree.

To recap, a gender pay gap related to any productive factor is the sum of two parts—gender differences in that factor and gender differences in the market returns to that factor. In the case of education, women have slightly more education than men in the United States, which should result in an overall pay ratio over 100 percent. Higher education for women, however, does not result in greater earnings as compared to men, as one would expect, but rather a pay ratio well below 100 percent since, for the same level of education, women receive lower compensation, as shown in Figure 5.4.

Can work hours explain the gender pay gap?

Another possible explanation for gender pay gaps is that, on average, women work fewer hours than men. In 2019, 23 percent of working women between the ages of twenty-five and sixty-four opted for part-time work, while this was the case for only 10 percent of men of the same ages. These patterns hold true across racial and ethnic groups, although to varying degrees, as seen in Figure 5.5. White and Hispanic workers exhibit the most "traditional" gender patterns of part-time and full-time work, with nearly one-quarter of working women and less than 10 percent of working men in part-time jobs. The smallest gender differential in part-time work is among Black women and men, with 19 and 13 percent working part-time, respectively. These race differences have their roots in decades-long patterns of work by Black men and women, prejudicial attitudes that can be

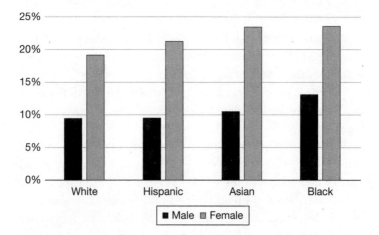

Figure 5.5 Percent of Workers Aged 25–64 Working Part-Time (Fewer than 35 Hours per Week) by Gender and Race

Source: 2019 ACS.

traced back to slavery, and within-race gender pay differentials. And while not as dissuaded from working by social norms as compared to white women, Black women face the double wage penalty of being both Black and female. In combination with lower earnings of potential Black male partners, the financial pressure to work more is evident both in labor force participation patterns and in a greater likelihood of full-time work.

Figure 5.6 shows the gender pay ratio between 1965 and 2019. The lower line shows the gender pay ratio for all US workers (aged sixteen and up) regardless of whether they work part-time or not. We can see that, even by 2019, all working women earn only slightly more than 70 percent of what all working men earn. When part-time (and part-year) workers are excluded from the calculation, we see the familiar pay ratio pattern in the upper line (repeated here from Figure 5.2). Because women are more likely to work part-time, the official pay ratio statistics are purposely calculated only for year-round, full-time workers.

While part-time work is not responsible for the size of the (year-round, full-time) pay ratio, it is still possible that there

Figure 5.6 Women's Median Earnings as a Percent of Men's for All Workers and for Year-Round, Full-Time Workers Aged 16 and Over

Source: US Census Bureau.

is a gender difference in hours worked even among men and women employed full-time. We typically think of a full-time workweek as forty hours, but that is not true for the average full-time worker in the United States. Even when we look only at full-time workers (defined by the BLS as working at least 35 hours per week), we see that male full-time workers average 45.1 hours per week, while female full-time workers average 42.5 hours per week. We expect that men, working about 5 percent more hours, have higher earnings as a result.

These differences in work hours have many root causes, including gender differences in occupational choice and family responsibilities. In professional occupations that are more predominantly male, like lawyer and manager, average weekly hours worked (47 hours per week and 46 hours, respectively) are higher than in more female-friendly occupations, like librarian and nurse (40 and 41 hours per week). Even within occupations, women work slightly fewer hours than men, but this is most noticeable among the highest-paying male-dominated occupations. For example, male physicians report working 54 hours per week on average, while female physicians report 52 hours per week. Similarly, patterns are evident among male (52 hours per week) and female (49 hours per week) lawyers. Gender differences in work hours among full-time workers are much smaller in female-dominated occupations; male librarians report working 30 minutes more per week than female librarians, and the difference for pre-school and elementary school teachers is only 20 minutes per week. The difference in hours between men and women full-time workers, both within and across occupations, is one factor that might explain some of the gender pay gap.

Can work experience explain the gender pay gap?

As discussed earlier, historically women have cycled in and out of the labor force. In the early 1900s, women's work often ceased with marriage, and many never returned to the labor force. In the middle of the twentieth century, women increasingly entered the workforce after they finished their schooling, then left to have children, and only returned when their children were older. By the turn of the century, many women worked continuously even as they raised their children, although it is still the case that a significant minority of women interrupt their careers to raise children. The result is that, on average, women have fewer years of work experience than men.

Work experience is valuable in the labor force. It allows workers to enhance their productivity, earn promotions, and advance their careers. Yet measuring exactly how much work experience individuals have is complicated and requires data beyond the ACS or the CPS. Fortunately, several longitudinal studies that follow women and men over time, such as the Panel Survey of Income Dynamics (PSID), allow us to get a fairly accurate measure of work experience. Since the PSID has been around for decades, we can compare work experience for women and men and examine changes over time.

A comparison of work experience for women and men using PSID data is shown in Figure 5.7. It is clear that over the decades, the gap in years of work experience has narrowed, some of which is due to men's decline in work experience. Although this difference has been decreasing, at least prior to the COVID-19 pandemic, the pandemic has the potential to once again widen the experience gap, since more women than men dropped out of the workforce to care for children.

Although the difference is decreasing, women still have lower levels of work experience due to more absences from the labor market. This variable helps explain one reason for the male advantage in the pay ratio. What is less apparent is that men receive greater compensation for each year of experience, and women have greater wage penalties for their absences.

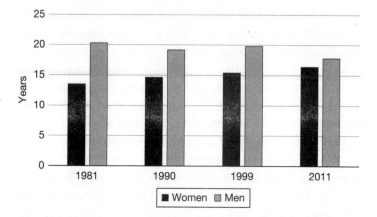

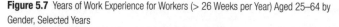

Figure 5.7 Years of Work Experience for Workers (> 26 Weeks per Year) Aged 25–64 by Gender, Selected Years

Source: Adapted from Blau, Francine D. and Lawrence M. Kahn. "The gender wage gap: Extent, trends, and explanations." *Journal of Economic Literature* 55 no. 3 (2017): 789–865.

Can family responsibilities explain the gender pay gap?

In the 1990s researchers highlighted the importance of family responsibilities as an explanation for the gender pay gap. In the United States in the early 1970s, the difference in earnings between working mothers and non-mothers (adjusted for age, education, marital status, and hours worked) was nearly 10 percent. In the late 1980s the gap began to narrow rapidly, and by 2013 it was less than 2 percent.[4]

That is not to say that the motherhood penalty is not large for certain groups. We can learn more from studies that analyze data from specialized groups of workers. For example, a study of the careers of MBA degree recipients who graduated from the University of Chicago between 1990 and 2006 revealed that although men and women started their post-MBA careers with roughly equal earnings, a mere five years after graduation their earnings trajectories diverged greatly, with men substantially out-earning women, and the differential grew over time.[5] Several factors explained most of this gap. Prominently, the presence of children was the main contributor to career interruptions and consequent slowing of the salary trajectory of female MBA graduates. MBA mothers had about eight months less work experience post-MBA than men, while childless MBA women had only a month and a half less work experience than MBA men. MBA mothers chose jobs that were family-friendly, with more predictable hours and consequently less room for advancement. The MBA mothers with higher-earning spouses were most likely to reduce their employment, whereas mothers with lower-earning spouses were less likely to reduce their employment after the birth of a child.

Similarly, professional women in Norway also faced a motherhood penalty. Most affected were women who had completed a graduate degree in one of four professional areas (business, law, medicine, or STEM) and who ranked among the top 20 percent of earners; they experienced lower earnings upon the birth of a child.[6] For men in the same occupations, the birth of a child did not slow down their wage growth at all. Although wage growth picks up again, only in STEM fields, and after ten years, do women's wages post-motherhood ever again approach those of men. The earnings drop for mothers was highest for those with an MBA or law degree and lowest for those in the sciences. Although men and women have children in equal proportions (for biological reasons if nothing else), the earnings implications are dramatically different.

Existing social norms may make it harder for mothers to stay in the highest-paying jobs. Some moms might find that they aren't offered certain opportunities—a job that requires significant travel or long hours, for example—because of the perception that they are the primary caregiver to a child. Women may also have strong preferences for providing the majority of care for their children and therefore cut back on work hours or even change occupations altogether. Whether or not this preference reflects prevailing social norms or is intrinsic to mothers—or both—is hard to discern. Interestingly, there is no fatherhood penalty to having children. Indeed, much research shows that men often experience a pay increase when they have children, seemingly benefiting from mothers assuming the majority of the childrearing responsibilities.

Can career differences explain the gender pay gap?

Wages are related to decisions that individuals make about their employment. They decide to work for employers within a particular industry, and their jobs are classified within a particular occupation. What exactly do these industry and occupation categories mean? More importantly, are these individual decisions related to the gender pay gap? Before we address these questions, some definitions are necessary.

An industry is a grouping of businesses that produce goods and or provide services that are related to one another. Although the Census Bureau identifies 290 detailed industrial categories, we will report on employers grouped into thirteen major industry sectors, including, for example, wholesale trade, construction, military, and a category that includes education, healthcare, and social assistance services.

While industrial classifications are based on the business an employer is in, occupation is about what job an employee performs. Like industry, there are many (over 900) very specific occupations, like preschool teacher and licensed vocational nurse, but these can be combined into much broader (and far fewer) categories. Though we will show some patterns for detailed occupations, we focus on twenty-three major occupational categories. Some examples of broad occupational categories include healthcare practitioners and food preparation and serving occupations. Although some occupations are likely to be closely linked to a particular industry, like healthcare practitioners working in the healthcare industry, it is important to recognize that many occupations are performed in different industries. For example, an accountant can work in the agricultural industry or in the finance industry. In fact, there are accountants working in every industry.

It is no secret that men and women are disproportionately represented in different industries and occupations. We have seen that some of this sorting can be attributed to the fact that many women with family responsibilities seek out jobs that require fewer hours and allow for more flexibility in work schedules.

Like much of what we have discussed so far, there are a few things that can help us understand the degree to which sorting into industries and occupations might exacerbate the gender pay gap. To contribute to the pay gap, it must be the case that wages differ across occupation (or industry) and that men are disproportionately represented in occupations and industries with the highest wages. On the other hand, occupation and industry patterns can also affect the pay gap if women and men in the same occupation and industry are paid differently. Let's take a look at all of that.

Are there gender pay differences within industries?

Because some industries provide goods and services in high demand or because they have work processes that make workers highly productive, their profit margins may allow for higher wages. Table 5.3 shows the percent of women, median pay by gender, and the pay ratio for year-round, full-time workers in the thirteen major industries, ranked in order from the lowest percent of female employees in 2019 to the highest. There is a great deal of variation in the representation of women across industries, from 9 percent in the construction industry to 72 percent in the education/healthcare/social assistance industry group.

Median earnings for men and women by industry do not follow a clear pattern in which male-dominated industries have exclusively higher median pay than those that are more balanced or female-dominated. In fact, male median earnings are highest in the finance/real estate and the professional/

Table 5.3 Percent Female Employment, Median Earnings, and Gender Pay Ratio for Year-Round, Full-Time Workers Aged 16 and Over by Industry

Industry	Percent Female	Men's Median Earnings	Women's Median Earnings	Ratio of Female to Male Median Earnings
Construction	9%	$49,497	$45,457	92%
Military	14%	$43,638	$44,850	103%
Agriculture, forestry, fishing/hunting, mining	18%	$48,487	$36,769	76%
Information	23%	$55,558	$43,436	78%
Retail trade	28%	$54,548	$45,457	83%
Wholesale trade	28%	$55,558	$41,012	74%
Finance/insurance, real estate	38%	$75,761	$60,609	80%
Services: professional/ scientific/technical/ management	40%	$70,710	$52,528	74%
Transportation/ warehousing, utilities	43%	$40,406	$30,910	76%
Public administration	44%	$69,700	$53,538	77%
Other service industries	44%	$42,426	$35,355	83%
Arts/entertainment/ recreation/accommodation/ food service	47%	$32,325	$28,284	87%
Services: education/ healthcare/social assistance	72%	$57,578	$45,457	79%

Source: 2019 ACS.

STEM/management industries, which are in the middle of the employee gender distribution at just about 40 percent female.

So what about relative pay *within* industries? Note that, with one exception, men out-earn women within each industry, and the two most male-dominated industries—construction and the military—have high pay ratios, 92 percent and 103 percent. In two industries that pay men well, finance/real estate and professional/STEM/management, the gender pay ratio for year-round, full-time workers is below the national average for all workers, at only 79 and 72 percent, respectively. Ironically, the service industry that employs the highest proportion of women, education/healthcare/social services, has a gender pay ratio that is no better, at 79 percent.

While firms in the same broad industry category serve similar markets for their goods and services and likely have similar profitability, it does not appear that those profits translate into equal earnings for their male and female employees. Keep in mind, though, that within a particular industry, women and men can be working in very different occupations.

Are there gender pay differences within occupations?

When looking at the causes of the gender pay gap, gender differences in occupation, referred to as occupational segregation, are an important consideration. With over 900 detailed occupational categories, it is clear that the work we do is diverse, but does it differ by gender? Gender differences in occupation across the entire economy are measured by the index of dissimilarity (first introduced in Chapter 2), which combines information about the gender composition in each of these occupations into a single indicator. This index identifies the proportion of women (or men) who would have to change occupations to achieve equal gender representation in every occupation. The index of dissimilarity has declined over time, from 70 percent in 1972 to its current level of about 50 percent, indicating that half of all workers would have to change occupation for there to be equal gender representation. It is clear that men and women are in different jobs, but what is important to our exploration of the gender pay gap is whether men and women are in jobs that pay substantially different salaries. Any systematic pattern of men working in high-paying occupations and women in low-paying occupations contributes to the pay gap. Even beyond that, it is possible that men and women are paid differently within a given occupation.

Table 5.4 Percent Female Employment, Median Earnings, and Gender Pay Ratio for Year-Round, Full-Time Workers Aged 16 and Over by Occupation

Occupation	Percent Female	Men's Median Earnings	Women's Median Earnings	Ratio of Female to Male Median Earnings
Construction and extraction	3%	$44,446	$35,355	80%
Installation, maintenance, and repair	4%	$50,507	$40,406	80%
Military	12%	$45,457	$45,760	101%
Architecture and engineering	15%	$86,872	$75,761	87%
Transportation and material moving	17%	$40,406	$28,284	70%
Farming, fishing, forestry	20%	$30,304	$23,132	76%
Protective service	21%	$56,568	$42,426	75%
Computer and mathematical operations	26%	$90,913	$75,761	83%
Production	27%	$43,133	$30,304	70%
Building and grounds cleaning and maintenance	35%	$30,910	$24,243	78%
Management	40%	$90,913	$66,670	73%
Sales	43%	$54,548	$35,355	65%
Arts, design, entertainment, sports, and media	45%	$60,609	$53,538	88%
Life, physical, and social sciences	46%	$75,761	$65,659	87%
Food preparation and serving	48%	$27,274	$23,233	85%
Legal	52%	$126,268	$70,710	56%
Business and financial operations	53%	$77,781	$61,619	79%
Community and social service	65%	$48,487	$46,467	96%
Educational instruction and library	72%	$60,609	$48,487	80%
Healthcare practitioners and technical	72%	$80,812	$60,609	75%
Personal care and service	72%	$33,335	$27,274	82%
Office and administrative support	73%	$43,032	$37,375	87%
Healthcare support	84%	$32,325	$30,304	94%

Source: 2019 ACS.

Table 5.4 shows the proportion of females, median earnings for men and women, and pay ratios for the twenty-three major occupation categories. We see that the proportion of women ranges from 3 percent of all employees in construction and extraction occupations to 84 percent of all employees in healthcare support occupations. Clearly neither of these are representative of the gender composition of the workforce overall, where women make up 43 percent of the year-round, full-time workforce. Does this occupational segregation contribute to the gender pay gap? Let's look at earnings.

There is considerable difference in the levels of earnings in various occupations. The lowest median earnings, regardless of gender, are among food preparation and service workers. Both men and women in food-related occupations earn less than $30,000 per year for year-round, full-time work—less than $15 per hour. In contrast, the legal profession, architecture/engineering, computing/mathematical operations, and management occupations all have a median income for male workers of over $85,000 per year (a whopping $126,268 in the legal profession). It is striking, then, to look at the proportion of women in these fields. Except for the legal profession, which is 52 percent female, women are in the minority in the other fields mentioned (architecture/engineering, 15 percent; computing/mathematical operations, 26 percent; management, 40 percent). It appears that the percentage of female workers is associated with the level of wages. This pattern of women in lower-paying occupations could explain much of the gender pay gap.

Even when women and men do the same work, they are generally not rewarded equally. In legal occupations, for example, women earn only 54 percent of what men earn. A substantial gender pay gap is evident in a number of other occupations: sales, transportation and material moving, and production have pay ratios that are no higher than 70 percent. On the other hand, in female-dominated occupations, women and men earn nearly identical wages: in the community and

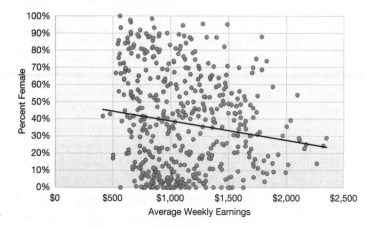

Figure 5.8 Female Share of Employment Versus Average Weekly Earnings for Full-Time Workers Aged 16 and Over, by Occupation

Source: 2019 CPS.

social services category, the pay ratio is 96 percent, and in the healthcare support occupations, it is 94 percent. In one case, the military, women even slightly out-earn men.

Although we see large variation even across these groupings, the true extent of occupational segregation may be masked by grouping so many detailed occupations into these twenty-three categories. To fully understand the relationship between occupation and earnings, we have plotted the median earnings in an occupation by the percent of an occupation that is female in Figure 5.8. Based on the trend line that is fitted among the individual data points for each occupation, it is clear that occupations with more women pay less. The highest-paying jobs are, by far, male-dominated, as shown in the lower right corner of the figure.

What do we make of this wealth of data on occupations and earnings? Women and men are not equally distributed across occupational categories, and those occupations that are disproportionately male have higher earnings. Unfortunately, even when men and women are in the same occupation they are not paid equally. The pay ratio for full-time workers within occupation nearly always lies below 100 percent.

Can union membership explain the gender wage gap?

We often assume that labor unions exist predominantly within the manufacturing industry. In reality, unions exist for many other jobs as well, and they can play an important role in equalizing pay differentials between men and women. This happens in part because unions adopt rigid rules about salaries, which minimizes managerial discretion in the salary determination process. Unions negotiate with management over salary and benefits in a process called collective bargaining.

Who is unionized? For this analysis, we turn to the CPS, which collects information on union representation. For men, one-fifth of unionized men work as teachers, firefighters, electricians, police officers, and truck drivers, but the remaining 80 percent are scattered throughout a wide variety of occupations. In contrast, just about one-half of women in unions work as nurses or in some type of educational capacity (e.g., teachers, education administrators, counselors, and social workers).

The impact of unionization on the gender pay gap can be divided into two parts. It is possible that men belong to unions (which increase pay) at higher rates than women. It is also possible that even if men and women are in unions at similar rates, the union pay boost may be higher for men than women.

So, what do the data tell us? It turns out that union membership is quite equal across gender, with 12.3 percent of women and 12.9 percent of men reporting union membership. Differences in union membership itself cannot be contributing to the gender pay gap.

Next, we compare the returns to men and women of belonging to a union. We noted that male and female union members are in quite different occupations, and in order to make a meaningful comparison about how much unions increase earnings, we need to net out the effect of occupation on wages as well as other factors affecting wages such as education, age, industry, and family status. Figure 5.9 shows the union wage premium by gender and race. The premium represents the excess earnings of union members compared to workers who are not in unions after netting out the aforementioned factors. With the exception of Asians, unionized workers benefit substantially from union membership in comparison to those in their own race/gender group who are not unionized. But, importantly, the benefits of unionization are not equal across groups. The premium is highest for unionized Hispanic men, who earn 16.1 percent more than otherwise similar Hispanic men who are not in unions. Black men have the next-highest premium, at 12.4 percent, followed by Black women, at 12.3 percent. White and Hispanic women have noticeably lower premiums at 5.8 and 9.4 percent, respectively. It is clear that unions boost pay for men more than for women, even after taking into account that unionized men and women work in different sectors of the economy. Overall, unions

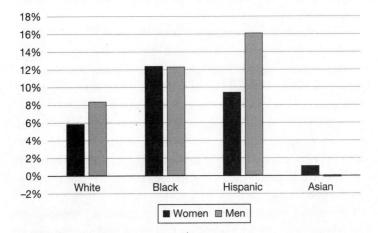

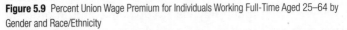

Figure 5.9 Percent Union Wage Premium for Individuals Working Full-Time Aged 25–64 by Gender and Race/Ethnicity

Source: 2019 CPS.

boost the pay of their female members on average 6.7 percent, whereas the figure is 9.9 percent for their male members.

Union membership is valuable to women who are represented by unions, compared to those that are not. However, union membership itself does not explain the gender pay gap, since men and women are nearly equally represented in unions. What does contribute to unequal pay between men and women is the fact that union wage-setting is more beneficial to male union members than to female union members.

How much of the gender pay gap do all of these measurable factors explain?

Underlying the gender pay ratio are two overarching causes for gender pay inequalities, leading us to ask: are women less productive than men, or are equally productive women paid less than their male counterparts? These questions require analysis more complicated than a simple ratio.[7] Remember, there is a group of worker characteristics that can be observed and that affect productivity. Let's say that we have data on individual male and female workers that includes individual pay and the following productivity variables: education, experience, work hours, occupation, and industry. And, for the sake of argument, let's say that the pay ratio for the whole population is 0.80 (that is, women are paid 20 percent less than men).

The first calculation is the portion of the pay gap that occurs because women have characteristics that are associated with lower productivity compared with the characteristics of men. In this example, that would be the wage loss if they had lower educational attainment, had less work experience, worked fewer hours, and/or were working in occupations and industries with lower pay. If they have lower productivity in at least some areas, it accounts for some of the observed pay gap. That portion is identified by using the results of regression analysis to calculate how much more women *would have been paid* if they had the same productivity as men. For the sake of argument, let's say that if we adjusted for these characteristics and considered lower pay for lower productivity "legitimate," then we could calculate the proportion of the 20 percent gap that is explained by productivity differences. If, in this example, 8 percentage points of the 20 percent gap can be explained by these factors, there are still 12 percentage points of the difference remaining. The second calculation is the "unexplained" portion of the gap. While it is equal to the remainder of the total gap, it also represents the pay difference even if women had the same productivity characteristics as men. Another way of thinking about it is that 40 percent (8/20) of the total pay gap is explained by productivity differences between men and women and the remaining 60 percent (12/20) is unexplained.

We calculated the explained and unexplained portions of the gender pay gap using data from the 2019 CPS. This survey has some advantages. It samples a large population and has detailed occupation and industry codes as well as information on education. It does not, however, have information on actual work experience. Still, as we showed earlier, the gap in men's and women's work experience has narrowed tremendously, meaning that we can use age as a somewhat imperfect measure of a worker's experience.

The results of these calculations are in Figure 5.10. The overall gender earnings ratio, unadjusted for any productivity factors, is 81 percent. Accounting for differences in age, race, state of residence, marital and child status, hours of work, and whether or not the survey respondent lives in a metropolitan area results in an adjusted pay ratio of 84 percent. It turns out that most of that improvement was due to differences in family status between men and women workers—working men are more likely to be married and have children than full-time working women. Adjusting for education, occupation, and industry raises the gender pay ratio even further. We know that women are more educated than men, and so the majority of this improvement, from 84 percent to 86 percent, is attributable to these detailed occupation and industry controls. This still

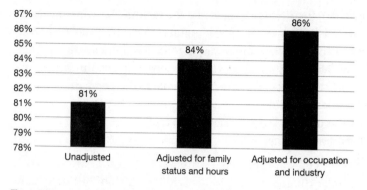

Figure 5.10 Women's Median Earnings as a Percent of Men's, Unadjusted and Adjusted for Productivity Factors for Full-Time Workers Aged 25–64

Source: 2019 CPS.

leaves a 14-percentage-point pay gap unexplained by productivity differences.

So how can we analyze this unexplained portion of the gender pay gap? This unexplained portion can represent different rewards to men and women for the same productivity. For example, men and women may have different rates of return for the same levels of education. Our analysis shows that women are paid less for their educational attainment—women receive salaries that are 1 percent lower than similarly educated men. Although this can be considered discrimination, it is not a direct measure because the unexplained portion can still reflect things that we cannot measure or that are difficult to measure. We discuss these remaining hard-to-measure factors in what follows. We caution that accounting for factors that could themselves result from discrimination can make the unexplained portion underrepresent the true level of discrimination.

What is left to explain the pay gap?

Our analysis above shows that observable variables that affect worker productivity and firm profitability explain part of the overall gender pay gap. While the factors that were measured in the CPS data raised the gender pay ratio from 81 percent to 86 percent, the remainder is considered unexplained. There are, however, some additional, hard-to-measure factors that differ by gender and may contribute to the gender pay gap.

Are women less likely to negotiate and are they less effective when they do?

We have established that a number of factors are related to gender differences in productivity on the job. But there is no magic formula that provides the exact wage that is deserved based on one's productivity. Productivity is not completely observable, and the process of setting wages usually involves some sharing of information and personal interactions between employers and employees. One important part of this is setting the starting salary when a worker is hired. In some instances, the pay is set when the job is listed. In others, particularly in professional jobs, there is a salary range, and the two parties have to negotiate to reach an agreement about the salary. Employers are motivated to minimize what they pay, while workers seek to maximize their pay. Often the employer makes an offer and the potential employee decides whether to accept or negotiate.

Negotiating typically involves making the case for an alternative salary offer and then deciding to accept (or not). Upon receiving a job offer, the standard advice is often to negotiate, to "lean in," yet many women opt not to. Is that a good strategy? Negotiating is viewed by long-standing cultural norms as a man's game. Men negotiate more often and more aggressively than women. More important, negotiation is expected from men and is socially compliant; from women, such an approach may be met with negative reactions and, consequently, less favorable outcomes.

Survey data indicate that working men are two to four times more likely to report negotiating for themselves than are working women.[8] Similarly, reports from new graduates receiving their master's degrees in business indicate that only 7 percent of female job seekers negotiated for a salary higher than the initial offer, compared to 57 percent of similar male job seekers. As a result, men were paid 7.6 percent more than women at the start of their careers.[9] These initial differences compound as the years go by, and the gap between men's and women's salaries grows.

The differences between men and women on the negotiating front are more nuanced than women simply preferring not to negotiate. Research indicates that the framing of the situation matters. If the process is framed as an opportunity to *ask* about additional salary instead of negotiating, the gender differences in salary discussions decline. On the other hand, when women aren't sure of their market value or whether they should negotiate, women may be more hesitant to do so than men. An intriguing experiment set out to test some of these assertions.[10] In this experimental study, participants were assigned roles as "workers" and "firms" and negotiated via anonymous chat messages. Both the workers and the firms were provided with information about the "market value" of the worker. There were two versions of the experiment: one in which workers were offered an initial wage and had to decide whether to accept it or enter negotiations, and a second in which workers received an initial wage offer but were required to negotiate.

When women in this experiment were asked to choose whether to negotiate, they were 11 percent less likely to enter negotiations than men. Digging into the details, the researchers found that when the offer was below their market value, women chose to negotiate 88 percent of the time, but when the offer was above their market value, only 44 percent chose to negotiate. This was in contrast to men, who negotiated more frequently even when the offer was above their market value. In the situation where women were required to negotiate, in 33 percent of their negotiations the wage actually decreased from the initial offer. The authors concluded that women opted out of negotiation situations that were likely to be costly, and that encouraging all women to negotiate might backfire for some. A cautionary tale for sure.

Even in the real world, "negotiating while female" does not always go well. Take, for instance, a study where men and women were sent out to negotiate the purchase of a new car. Male and female actors were sent to car dealerships, dressed similarly, and armed with identical credit ratings, employment, and homeownership details on their credit applications. After following very precise (and identical) negotiating scripts, white women ended up paying 1 percent more and Black women 3 percent more than white men for the same new car.[11]

Negotiating in a professional setting is very different for men than for women. According to conventional wisdom, for women, negotiation is seen as an improper act of appearing greedy. It is frowned upon by many women, who are often intimidated or embarrassed by the act of asking to be compensated for their value in the workplace. The same is not true for men, who are encouraged, even expected to ask—in keeping with gender norms. Being less inclined to negotiate, and facing smaller gains when they do, sets women back in their starting salaries and raises, which contributes eventually to large salary gaps. As part of their quest for gender salary equity, some large companies have eliminated the possibility of negotiation for all employees—new hires and existing employees alike. Perhaps this is an important step along the way to closing the gender pay gap.

Are women less competitive than men and can it help explain the gender pay gap?

You have probably been led to believe that men are more competitive than women and that this may contribute to the gender pay gap. Those who are more competitive may thrive in an environment where comparisons between workers are important. For example, firms often require workers to compete with each other to earn promotions because there are fewer positions at the top of the corporate ladder. There are some circumstances where pay or bonuses are determined by head-to-head performance (e.g., the highest-performing sales representative gets the largest bonus).

Two classic experiments in economics have established that women are less likely to engage in competitions and that when they do compete, they do not perform as well as men. These experiments involved men and women—usually college students—who complete tasks such as solving mazes or adding sets of numbers and are compensated based on their performance. When participants are rewarded based on their own performance (piecework pay), men and women perform the same—they are equally productive. This is important because it establishes that men and women are equally able to complete the tasks. The experiment then turned to a winner-take-all reward structure where only the highest performing person gets paid. This is sometimes called "tournament pay," and it is very common in the corporate world, where, for example, many individuals compete for promotion to one slot. Under the winner-take-all pay scheme, men's performance increases while women's stays the same.

In a related experiment in which men and women could choose whether to be compensated under piecework or tournament pay, women chose piecework more often than men. Even men who performed below average tended to choose a tournament reward scheme; in this case, economists concluded that the men were overconfident. The results of these experiments are taken to indicate that women do not perform as well as men under competitive pressure and are less interested in competitive environments. However compelling these findings are, we still do not have definitive evidence on how competitiveness affects the gender earnings gap because large data sets on earnings typically do not include information on competitiveness.

Are women more risk-averse than men?

Individuals' views about risk can affect their salaries if they prefer to minimize taking physical or financial risks that can't be avoided in some occupations. Particularly dangerous occupations—for example, roofer or machine operator— or jobs that involve making risky decisions about financial investments that gain or lose millions of dollars are not for everyone. But it is often the case that such jobs, compared to others that require similar education and experience, pay more. This is called a compensating wage differential, so gender differences in risk-taking can contribute to pay differences.

Economists rely on experimental research to measure gender differences in risk aversion. In these studies, which are focused largely on financial risk, men and women are asked to choose between options that pay them a guaranteed amount and a "lottery" that may have the same payout on average but, to varying degrees, the probability of a much higher or lower payout based on chance. Nearly all of the studies find that women are more risk-averse than men, in that they are more likely to choose the guaranteed amount. Other studies offer "investment" choices with a variety of ranges of possible gains and losses. Although these choices have the same average rate of return, the amount that could be gained (or lost!) is much higher among the riskier options. When faced with these choices, women are consistently more risk-averse than men. In particular, women are wary of situations in which there is the chance of a large loss. What is interesting is that, as with many of the behaviors we have considered, women behave differently as the framing of the decision changes. In one experiment, for example, women are shown to be more risk-averse when a decision is referred to as "gambling" than when they are asked to make decisions described as investments or buying insurance.

So how might this difference in risk-taking affect the gender pay gap? Risk aversion has been linked to differences in outcomes such as educational and occupational choices as well as financial decision-making. In education, risk preferences predict how one goes about answering questions on standardized exams. Risk aversion, particularly among women, has been found to reduce willingness to guess and to increase the time spent deciding among answers to multiple-choice questions, often resulting in lower scores.[12] Higher levels of risk-taking even seem to be related to choosing majors in the STEM fields. It is not difficult to imagine how risk preferences, combined with these educational choices, may lead to observable differences in occupation and pay that favor men.

Women exhibit risk aversion to financial decision-making insofar as they select less risky investment portfolios and are less likely to make frequent stock trades, resulting in lower overall levels of wealth. This is not reflected in the gender pay gap, which focuses on labor-market earnings, but this lower wealth is compounded by the fact that women earn lower incomes and thus have less overall to invest. Taken together, these behaviors and labor force realities can have major impacts on available income in retirement—particularly worrisome given that on average women live longer than men.

Are there biological differences between men and women that contribute to the pay gap?

There are long-held views that women are not biologically suited for certain types of work. In response, many countries have banned women from employment in some occupations. Even in the United States, in industries that employ nearly one-quarter of the workforce, such as mining, manufacturing, public safety, and the military, tests of physical ability are part of the hiring process. Since men are on average stronger and have greater cardiovascular stamina, it is important to ensure that what is being tested truly matches job requirements. The EEOC has focused on precisely this issue and made it costly for employers who use inappropriate hiring standards. In 2018, a freight company settled with female applicants for more than $3 million because of inequitable physical tests after an initial lawsuit filed by the EEOC. Some employers are taking proactive stances to improve their number of female employees despite legitimate physical job requirements.

There have long been discussions of women's unsuitability for difficult work; it seems ironic that women are considered delicate, despite having lower mortality at all ages and greater longevity than men throughout the world. To cite one egregious example, in 1995, on the topic of women serving in the military, the *New York Times* famously quoted Speaker of the House Newt Gingrich as saying, "Females have biological problems staying in a ditch for 30 days because they get infections, and they don't have upper body strength."[13] This degree of ignorance of basic human biology, especially from a public official in the late twentieth century, is as stunning as it is harmful to women's rights to equal pay.

Two male economists set out to test something akin to Gingrich's assertion.[14] They suggested that part of the gender pay gap resulted from more absences from work due to women's menstrual cycles. To test this hypothesis, they used data from personnel records of a large Italian bank and reported that absences from work for women followed a regular twenty-eight-day pattern. Subsequent work by other economists to replicate these results, an important hallmark of the scientific method, demonstrated that these particular findings were sensitive to some minor coding errors and methodological choices; when the analysis was extended to employers other than just a single Italian firm, researchers found no such results.[15]

There are other, more complex ways in which sex-based biological differences have been implicated in labor market outcomes. Research at the intersection of biology and economics is still in the early stages, but some of this research suggests that biology, including hormones, genetics, and brain functioning, plays a role in economic behaviors. There is much more work to be done, however, to determine if these sex-based biological differences contribute to the gender pay gap.

Finally, relatively new interdisciplinary research that combines neuroscience, psychology, and economics examines what happens in the brain when decisions are made. Though links between the brain's neural systems and computational processing and one's actual decision-making have been found, this type of research has not yet been used to understand gender differences in economic decision-making and possible contributions to gender pay differentials. It will be interesting to see what these innovative lines of research reveal.

6

DO WOMEN EARN LESS BECAUSE MEN RULE THE WORLD?

Measuring the gender pay ratio and exploring underlying causes for the gap between women's and men's rates of pay revealed some justifiable reasons for gender pay differences. Yet even after accounting for measurable productivity factors, gender pay differences remain. This unexplained residual is sometimes described as a measure of pay discrimination, but the issue is not that simple. There are a number of reasons pay discrimination is particularly difficult to quantify. In this chapter we define discrimination and then explore several theories aimed at explaining the causes of such discrimination. Understanding the source of discrimination against women in the labor market is crucial for designing policies to eradicate it. Following a discussion of the techniques used to measure discrimination, the chapter concludes with a summary of the evidence regarding gender-based discrimination in the labor market.

What exactly is labor market discrimination?

The definition of "discriminate" in the *Oxford English Dictionary* is to "make an unjust or prejudicial distinction in the treatment of different categories of people, especially on the grounds of ethnicity, sex, age, or disability." A great deal is contained in that definition. Let's unravel it a bit.

It won't surprise you to know that economists, with our penchant for measuring things, define discrimination in a very particular way: based on observable outcomes. Specifically, labor market discrimination occurs if labor market outcomes for two equally productive (or qualified) individuals differ based on their group identity. Typically the group identities that would be included in this list are those that are mentioned under Title VII of the 1964 Civil Rights Act, which as amended specifically prohibits labor market discrimination based on race, color, religion, sex, national origin, age, veteran status, pregnancy, or disability. And while those are the legal categories of discrimination, there are other group identities that can result in differential labor market outcomes, such as appearance, political affiliation, marital status, and parental responsibilities, among others.[1] As for the rest of the definition, labor market outcomes can include important aspects of work such as who gets hired, how much workers are paid in salary and benefits, who gets promoted or laid off, and other decisions that affect a worker's earnings and career trajectory.

To understand the gender pay gap, we focus on labor market discrimination that occurs if equally productive individuals are paid differently based on their gender. Keep in mind, however, that other types of labor market discrimination can play a role by distorting which workers are viewed as equally productive. For example, if equal productivity includes working in a position with the same job title, then differences in hiring and promotion may, in fact, cause potentially equally productive women to appear less productive than men, and any resulting pay differences might not be measurable as discrimination. It is even the case that discrimination that affects labor market outcomes may occur before an individual enters the labor market—for example, if individuals receive unequal quality of education in the public school system or are discouraged from attending college or pursuing particular fields of study.

What causes pay discrimination?

Economists use models to understand pay discrimination within labor markets where the competing forces of the supply of and demand for labor determine the equilibrium wage. This section discusses well-known theoretical models that explain many causes of pay discrimination. Insights from these theories—and any statistical evidence that supports or refutes them—help policymakers understand how to combat pay discrimination.

Do biases against women cause pay discrimination?

The first economist to seriously tackle the issue of pay discrimination was Gary Becker, the 1992 recipient of the Nobel Memorial Prize in Economic Sciences. Focused largely on what Becker called "tastes for discrimination" against racial and ethnic minorities, his theory has also been used to help explain discrimination on the basis of sex. Discrimination is rooted in prejudice that the majority (in this case, white men) might have toward minority workers (people of color and women, among others). Becker's model posits that the prejudicial views (a subjective dislike for a group of workers or at least a distaste of their presence in the workplace) held by majority group employers, fellow employees, or even customers can have an impact on the pay or workplace position of equally qualified minority workers. Let's take a closer look.

Can pay discrimination occur if employers are prejudiced toward women?

Employers (owners and managers) with the power to hire, determine salaries, and make decisions about other important aspects of a job may treat women differently based on their own preferences. According to Becker's model, if an employer has a subjective dislike of women in the workplace, it is personally costly to them to have women working at the company. To accommodate these preferences, prejudiced employers will increase their demand for male workers and decrease demand for female workers. As employers compete for male workers in the labor market, the wage rate paid to male workers rises. The lower demand for female workers drives their wage down, and equally productive women receive lower pay than men—the very definition of pay discrimination. In this model, in order for women to be hired, there must be a pay gap sufficient to entice prejudiced employers to hire women workers. Those employers who do not hire women will have lower profits because they hire the more expensive men.

But there is more to this taste-for-discrimination theory. Markets are often praised for their efficiency. Through competition, wages should be determined by worker productivity. How, then, could equally productive male and female workers be paid differently? Becker's model highlights the fact that non-discriminating employers, with no particular preferences for male or female workers, will respond to the lower wages paid to female employees by seeking them out to hire. This raises the demand for female workers, and if there are enough non-prejudiced employers, wages for female workers will rise to the point of pay equality. Ironically, this model, intended to explain pay discrimination, concludes with the idea that it will be eliminated as long as there are enough non-discriminating employers and firms operate in a market with considerable competitive pressures to keep costs down. However, employers in markets with little competition may be able to absorb the higher costs associated with indulging their taste for discrimination, and in such cases market forces will not eliminate the pay differential. Hence, although this model is used by some policymakers and businesses to argue that we do not need laws against pay discrimination, we caution that this conclusion of Becker's theory rests on assumptions that are seldom, if ever, met in practice.

Although overt bias against women is not as strong as it was in the past, there is still reason for concern. Evidence indicates that women are hired into managerial positions at lower rates, receive less favorable work evaluations, and are less likely to be promoted than men. For example, one study of performance evaluations showed that women were viewed differently than equally qualified men by their supervisors. Because of the subjective nature of many performance reviews, the same accomplishments or behaviors can be described with a positive spin or a negative one, and researchers found that evaluations for women employees were often more critical, particularly when the evaluations were conducted by male supervisors.[2] Further studies, discussed later, are necessary to see if this employer prejudice manifests itself in differential hiring and pay in the labor market.

Can pay discrimination occur if male employees dislike working with female co-workers?

What if co-workers are prejudiced against working with women in the workplace? This prejudice would play out differently than in the case of employer prejudice. Even though prejudiced employees do not directly control the demand for labor (and hence wages), their preferences do have an impact on overall productivity in the workplace. Extensions to Becker's original model suggest that women in a workplace with co-workers prejudiced against working with them can cause lower workplace productivity among the prejudiced co-workers. This in turn lowers the demand for women in male-dominated workplaces, based on their lower contribution to overall productivity. Rather than pay discrimination, the most likely result from this type of employee-prejudice-based discrimination would be gender-segregated workplaces. In this case, markets may sort workers into the most efficient locations or even occupations through segregation, whether fair to workers or not.

So is there evidence that there is a preference for male co-workers? Recent surveys of workers indicate that the overwhelming majority do not express a preference for male or female colleagues. While it is heartening that most workers have no gender preferences, when men do have a preference they prefer to work alongside men, suggesting that employee biases may contribute to occupational segregation. It is puzzling that women who express a preference also prefer to work alongside men. Increasingly personnel offices are turning to anti-bias training in an attempt to reduce prejudices that fuel labor market discrimination.

Can pay discrimination occur if customers prefer not to interact with women?

The final economic decision-maker of Becker's three models is the case where it is customers who are prejudiced against women in the workplace. In this version of the theory, it is assumed that even if neither employers nor employees are negatively affected by the presence of female workers, customers are. There is evidence from surveys that, even today, customers prefer not to have women pilots, lawyers, or even chefs. If this is the case, then the employers (the airline, law firm, or restaurant) will see their business drop off when they hire female employees, and these firms may have to lower their prices to appease customers. Even though non-discriminating employers themselves do not care, and non-discriminating co-workers would remain equally productive, the firm's profits are lower due to the decrease in business when the firm employs women, unless the women are in positions where they do not have customer contact.

Unlike the models of employer and employee tastes for discrimination, there is no market mechanism to offset this type of discrimination. The demand for female workers simply falls and their wages follow suit. Since this is the only one of Becker's models of pay discrimination that is not expected to fade away through the workings of the market, it has generated data-driven studies that investigate whether customer biases exist. Of course, in order to conduct such a test, a researcher would need some way of determining what a customer likes or doesn't like. In one example, a group of researchers turned to a huge database that provides customer ratings of male and female employees: the ratings of Uber drivers by their passengers. There are only small differences in productivity: women have slightly less experience and drive at slightly slower speeds on average. After accounting for those factors, ratings of male and female drivers were not found to be significantly different.[3]

That is not the case in other work settings. It is well known at colleges and universities that male professors and instructors receive better student evaluations on average than do comparable female faculty. In addition, a survey of customer ratings (and tips) at restaurants in Virginia reveals that ratings of the service provided by female servers (and the corresponding tips) are lower than for male servers, a pattern particularly evident among male diners. This descriptive evidence suggests that customers in many work settings, particularly those where there is face-to-face contact between the employee and the customer, have a preference for male employees. Studies that carefully control for productivity differences and the impact of customer biases on earnings are needed to understand if these preferences translate into meaningful pay discrimination.

Does gender pay discrimination occur because employers are hedging their bets without information about how productive women will be?

In economic theory, firms are assumed to make decisions about hiring workers and setting initial salaries with the goal of maximizing profit. The demand for labor represents the firm's willingness to pay for worker productivity, while the supply of labor represents the value that workers require to give up their non-market time to work at the firm.

This model presumes that the firm knows how productive each worker will be, but of course that is not likely to be the case. At the time they are choosing which applicant to hire, an employer can observe some productivity factors, such as the level of education and past work history, but they would also like to know which employees are likely to be the easiest to train, the most productive, the most reliable, or the most committed to the firm. The worker knows a great deal about their own skill and commitment, but the potential employer does not. In this case of asymmetric information, employers will often resort to using the average characteristics of a group to infer the productivity of an individual who is a member of that group. This form of profiling is referred to as "statistical discrimination." Without accurate information about individual productivity and commitment, which is likely to be costly to discern, the best an employer can do is to use these average characteristics to fill in the gaps. Assumptions about productivity can be based on a wide range of observable information, like the college attended, the length of time it took to get a degree, race or nationality, and of course gender.

A profit-maximizing firm might engage in statistical discrimination based on gender if it has imperfect information and cannot be certain about each individual's productivity. For example, firms might draw on experience that indicates that women are more likely to have labor force reductions or absences when faced with increasing family responsibilities— just think of how many women ended up dropping out of the labor force to care for children during the COVID-19 pandemic. These firms might resort to gender-based statistical discrimination to increase productivity. If firms are looking to hire people into jobs where there are considerable training costs, the employer may believe that a particular woman is qualified for the job, but may worry that she will not make the long-term commitment necessary for a firm's investment in her training to pay off. It will be difficult to verify whether any particular applicant will stay with the firm for the long haul (and under many circumstances it is not legal to ask). A simple solution to this lack of information, from the firms' perspective, may be to offer jobs to men, who can more predictably be expected to have a stronger attachment to the labor force. This preference for male workers is reflected in an increase in demand, which in turn translates into more job offers and potentially higher starting salaries for men than for women. How can we tell if statistical discrimination rather than personal prejudice is the explanation for gender pay differentials?

Theory suggests that pay differences will be permanent if customer prejudice is the underlying cause, as compared to increases in relative pay that should occur as employers learn more about actual productivity and discontinue their reliance on group membership as an imperfect indicator of an individual's productivity. Researchers find patterns of wages and initially hard-to-observe productivity characteristics that are consistent with statistical discrimination, but the relatively small number of studies of these gender wage patterns prevents making sweeping statements about the degree of gender-based statistical discrimination.

As a means to inform effective anti-discrimination policy, it is important to remember the conditions that lead to statistical discrimination. It is not because employers (or others) actively dislike female applicants; it is because profit-maximizing employers are relying on inaccurate stereotypes or outdated information to make hiring and salary-setting decisions. Unlike cases in which prejudice must be combatted, statistical discrimination can be addressed by making available more accurate, up-to-date information about the true productivity of women in the workplace and encouraging applicants to provide more detailed productivity information in job applications.

Is occupational crowding a form of pay discrimination?

Noted feminist economist Barbara Bergmann highlighted another cause of pay differentials called "occupational crowding." Occupational crowding occurs when women are limited to a relatively small subset of occupations that are deemed appropriate for their gender based on societal norms. Such crowding results in an increase in the supply of labor in these female-dominated occupations, and if there are few available occupations and a large number of female workers, wages for these workers will be low.

There is no doubt that there is a great deal of gender-based occupational segregation in the United States. Though it has slowly declined, the index of dissimilarity remains at about 50 percent, and on average, wages in occupations that are predominantly female lie well below wages in predominantly male occupations. This sorting into low-paying occupations can account for some of the gender pay gap, but it is clear that gender differences in occupation don't fully explain the gap. Within the same occupation, men are nearly always paid more than women.

While barriers to women's access to certain jobs that existed in the nineteenth and early twentieth centuries might explain how occupational crowding originated, such legal barriers have since been removed. So occupational segregation is related to gender differences in pay, but is occupational crowding really discrimination? Perhaps not. If women's crowding into a small group of occupations is simply the result of their choices, then it is not discrimination. But, of course, there is an entire series of choices that culminate in a woman's eventual occupation. First, she decides how far to go in school. At each step in her schooling, she decides what to study. Armed with educational skills, she then pursues a job and must match up with an employer willing to hire her. The key to determining if occupational segregation is discrimination is if men and women with equal productivity or potential are treated differently. If, at each step in this progression, the choice is made entirely voluntarily, then occupational segregation is not discrimination. If, on the other hand, these decisions are the result of barriers faced by women—and, importantly, not by men—in terms of societal expectations and unequal opportunities or treatment as they move through education and into the workplace, then this is indeed a form of discrimination. You can see the inherent difficulty in determining if crowding is truly voluntary. Research in the area of hiring into specific occupations will help us understand if there are discriminatory barriers to women's occupational choices.

Why is it so hard to measure discrimination?

The definition of pay discrimination leads us to the heart of the problem in measuring it. The difficulty is that we have to compare equally productive individuals. As we saw in Chapter 5, there are a number of productivity characteristics that we can observe, but even those are just indicators of productivity. In order to determine if discrimination has occurred, we need to measure the total productivity of an individual and what those characteristics are worth to a firm. The task is daunting.

There are a few instances where productivity is observable, like when workers produce a single product and are paid a piece rate for each item that they produce. Few of us work in that environment. To use ourselves as an example, as authors of this book, together we have produced a product that is tangible and can be measured. We also co-edited an earlier book about women in economics and produced co-authored journal articles. But we teach at different universities, our classes differ in size and level, and our students take away varying degrees of understanding of economics. Perhaps most difficult of all, we also attend meetings where we work with groups of other employees to develop policies and new programs to benefit the employees and students at our respective universities. With such varied output, how can we accurately measure whether one of us is more productive than the other? Worse yet, how can an employer discern at the moment that we're hired (and our starting salary is set) how productive we each will be? Of course they can't accurately predict our future productivity. And in most cases, researchers have no way of measuring either actual or potential productivity. Economists and researchers in other disciplines have adopted a variety of techniques to try to address the difficulties inherent in measuring discrimination.

How do we measure discrimination?

There are a variety of approaches to measure the extent of labor market discrimination in general, and pay discrimination of women in particular. Each method has limitations, but the body of research as a whole can help us understand if there is sufficient evidence that discrimination plays a role in the differences between women's and men's labor market outcomes. Below we explain the most common methods of measuring discrimination.

What can we learn about discrimination from the Oaxaca-blinder decomposition?

Many studies rely on the regression-based Oaxaca-Blinder decomposition to statistically measure discrimination. Recall that this approach, first presented in Chapter 5, begins with the observed gender pay ratio for year-round, full-time workers and then accounts for as many measurable productivity characteristics as possible, using data from large surveys of individuals. Typically, after accounting for measurable productivity characteristics, the explained ratio rises, but there is still a residual unexplained pay gap. This residual is sometimes referred to as a measure of discrimination.

For this residual to give us meaningful insights into the degree of discrimination, the onus is on the researcher to answer two questions. First, did the decomposition model include information on *all* productivity differences between men and women? If so, the unexplained portion can be interpreted as discrimination. Of course, there is a long list of things that might affect productivity that might not be available for this type of analysis, and this approach is open to criticism, particularly to those ideologically inclined to refute the existence of discrimination. Most notably, those inclined to refute the possibility of discrimination suggest that if a model fails to include some productivity measures that indicate that women are less productive than men, then the unexplained gap is simply a reflection of these omitted productivity characteristics rather than discrimination. Even the most careful researcher may not be able to include all appropriate variables due to limitations in the data.

A second problem with the decomposition approach stems from including too many, rather than too few, productivity characteristics. What if the productivity adjustment included something that itself is the result of discrimination? For example, if a job title is used to draw equivalence in productivity between men and women, but if women are discriminated against in the promotion process, we might find that a sizable portion of the pay gap is explained by job title. Using the job title variable in the decomposition of the pay ratio, however, and legitimizing it as a productivity difference results in an underestimation of the role of labor market discrimination in gender pay gaps.

With these caveats in mind, the unexplained residual of a carefully conducted Oaxaca-Blinder decomposition sheds light on the magnitude of gender-based pay discrimination. Because one can never prove that the exactly appropriate characteristics have been included, the results of such a decomposition can be open to differing interpretations by arguing that too few or too many variables have been included.

In Chapter 5, we saw the results of decomposition analysis conducted with the CPS data from 2019 in Figure 5.10. The unadjusted wage ratio indicated that the average year-round, full-time female worker earned 81 percent of the average year-round, full-time male worker's earnings, for an initial pay gap of 19 percentage points. Using the decomposition method, and accounting for productivity differences in family status (marriage and children) and work hours (even among full-time workers), the explained pay ratio increased to 84 percent—leaving an unexplained gap of 16 percentage points. Adding the final set of work-related productivity variables that included gender differences in education, occupation, and industry, the final pay ratio was 86 percent. The remaining 14 percentage points of the pay gap represent what is left unexplained once all of these productivity differences are accounted for.

Of course, this does not prove how much discrimination remains. There may still be other productivity factors not included in the data that explain part of that gap. In fact, we acknowledged that the CPS data do not provide information on work experience. Evidence suggests that previous work experience typically is greater for men and is associated with higher wages. This makes work experience a contributing factor to the remaining pay gap in our example. We can look at a decomposition from another national data set, albeit from more than a decade ago, that included information on prior work experience.[4] Because men of equal age have slightly more years of full-time work experience in the labor market than women (1.4 years more on average), this additional work experience closes the pay gap by an additional 4 percentage points. If we assume that the amount of work experience for men and women and the return to it have not changed since 2010, then the inclusion of gender differences in experience in the 2019 CPS decomposition model further reduces the unexplained gap to around 10 percentage points. It is possible that this entire gap is due to discrimination.

Can experiments in a lab help us measure discrimination?

Experiments conducted in a lab have been used to test for discriminatory decision-making and to gain an understanding of the type of discrimination that might be driving differences in labor market outcomes. Research subjects are recruited to come to a research site, typically a computer lab, where they are provided with information and asked to make a series of decisions. The researcher controls the information that the subjects are given; in our examples they are often provided with productivity information or a description of a detailed work scenario and the gender of the (fictitious) workers. They are then asked to make decisions about, for example, hiring, firing, promoting, or setting salaries for the worker(s). If this experiment is set up well, administered properly, and presents equally productive workers, any differential treatment is, by definition, discrimination.

Many lab studies report negative outcomes for women as compared to men, although there are some differences linked to the occupation and context of the scenario and the gender of the research subject. One early study recruited bank managers attending a management institute as research subjects.[5] These subjects were provided a number of documents describing various scenarios, including different job demands, expected qualifications, work hours, and employee performance. Subjects were asked to make decisions regarding promotion, professional development, disciplinary action, and requests for leave for these hypothetical workers. The sex of the worker and circumstances of the situation were manipulated by the researcher in multiple scenarios.

In one scenario, these bank managers were given a memo that described an employee being considered for promotion. The job details were presented as either complex or routine and job candidates identified as either male or female. After reviewing the information, subjects were asked to recommend the candidate for promotion and also to rate the candidate on their skills in the areas of customer relations and employee management. The results indicated that male administrators were less likely to promote and train and more likely to discipline female employees.

A number of other lab experiments both in the United States and in other countries have been conducted with somewhat mixed results, but many of these point to discrimination against women. This aligns with the findings from lab experiments that focused on differential outcomes when men and women negotiate for salary and engage in self-promotion.

The primary concern with lab experiments is what is called "external validity." In other words, can a researcher provide information and ask a subject to make decisions that truly mimic those made in a real work setting? Care needs to be taken in designing experiments to emulate workplace decisions as much as possible.

What do we gain by moving experiments outside of the lab?

The problem of external validity can be addressed by situating an experiment in the actual work setting. Field studies provide detailed information about fictitious applicants for jobs to real-world decision-makers.

There are two general types of field studies, correspondence studies and audit-pair studies. A researcher conducting a correspondence study sends out fictitious applications and resumes in response to job postings. The applications will be similar, but not identical, in all ways that signal productivity and commitment. In most studies that investigate gender discrimination, applications include names that are typically associated with females or males (think Nancy or Sharon as compared to Michael or Steven). Along with many actual applications for a job, the applications for fictitious job-hunters are received by the person charged with the job search at the firm and go through the application review process. The outcome in this type of experiment is whether or not an applicant receives a callback for an interview, and because the applicant information is essentially identical, differences in callback rates between female and male applicants would reflect discrimination.

The second type of field experiment is called an audit-pair study. Researchers arrange for real people to pose as applicants who are intended to be nearly identical in every way and go through the hiring process with actual employers and in competition with actual applicants. The difference here is that the process goes beyond the paper/online application phase and involves interviews with the potential employer either by phone or in person. The same care must be taken with the application materials as in a correspondence study, but in addition, actors must be trained to have equivalent interactions with the potential employer. This involves careful attention to dress, grooming, and speech, and often carefully crafted instructions for verbal interactions, among other important considerations. The outcome for these audit-pair studies is typically a job offer.

Field experiments have provided evidence of discrimination against women. An audit-pair study that sent male and female testers out on job interviews for positions as servers at restaurants in Philadelphia found hiring discrimination against both women and men in different work settings.[6] In keeping with the pay differences we see throughout the economy, women were less often hired at expensive restaurants (where servers' earnings are higher) but favored in hiring at lower-priced establishments. Many of the studies in this area look at hiring discrimination in occupations that are predominantly male (e.g., accountant and auto mechanic) and others that are predominantly female (e.g., secretary and waitstaff). In general, these studies find that women face hiring discrimination in male-dominated occupations while men face hiring discrimination in female-dominated occupations. Because average earnings tend to be higher in male-dominated occupations, these findings suggest that this pattern of hiring discrimination contributes to the overall gender pay gap. In addition, these results lend support to the notion that some portion of occupational segregation, and the resulting pay differences caused by occupational crowding, are not entirely voluntary but are partly the result of discrimination.

Another study sent similar nearly identical fictitious resumes for women, with some randomly assigned an LGBTQ indicator.[7] To signal sexual orientation on the treatment resumes, a woman was listed as a leader in a campus LGBTQ association, which presumably allowed hiring managers to infer that the woman was a member of the LGBTQ community. For the control resumes, women held a secretarial position at a student organization with progressive views. After accounting for other factors affecting hiring, the researchers determined that listing a leadership role in an LGBTQ organization on a woman's resume lowered her odds of being contacted by an employer by 32.5 percent.

A study that examines the motherhood penalty, the penalty for a perceived lack of commitment, effort, and reliability on the part of mothers toward their employers, conducts both a lab experiment of scenarios regarding employees and a field study of job candidates.[8] A series of candidates (parents and non-parents, men and women) were assigned equal productivity through a detailed resume and summary from a fictitious human resources department. Then laboratory subjects were asked to rate the candidates and recommend hiring and salary. Interestingly, women candidates were rated higher on commitment and competence, but this gender advantage was more than erased by a motherhood penalty. Mothers were rated lower and awarded salaries more than $10,000 lower than non-mothers. Fathers, on the other hand, were rated better and were awarded higher salaries than non-fathers. Mothers were least likely to be recommended for promotion and management training.

One of the advantages of both the lab and field experiments just described is that the researcher has the ability to manipulate the information provided in order to test alternative theories of discrimination. Most test the model of statistical discrimination—that is, that discrimination will be reduced as more information about individual productivity is provided. The setup is straightforward: to test gender discrimination, some applications (or audit pairs) are sent out with minimal information about education and other productivity data, leaving the hiring team to fill in the gaps—potentially with what they may or may not know about the average productivity of men and women. Other applications and pairs are sent with much greater detail,

leaving little doubt as to the relative productivity of the fictitious applicants. Results from these studies indicate that hiring
decisions are favorable to men when information is minimal but
that the hiring gap between men and women declines as more
information is provided. This is consistent with the model of statistical discrimination and suggests that additional information
can be a powerful deterrent to gender discrimination in hiring.

Experimental studies have also explored the notion that
statistical discrimination against women arises specifically because of concerns about lack of commitment or productivity
declines related to *future* family responsibilities. This type of
statistical discrimination against women has been tested in a
correspondence study of jobs in the French financial sector.
In this study, applications were sent out for individuals with
varying probabilities of future childbearing or child-rearing
responsibilities. There were three groups of both male and
female applicants: age twenty-five, unmarried and childless;
age thirty-seven, unmarried and childless; and age thirty-
seven, married with three children. If employers are concerned
about work disruptions from future childbearing, lower rates
of hiring would be expected for women in the first group of
applicants. These researchers did not find significant overall
differences in callback rates by gender in any of the groups
when they examined hiring in all types of finance jobs. When
they looked separately at finance jobs that require higher
qualifications or substantial employer-provided training, they
found that young, unmarried, childless women received fewer
callbacks than identical male applicants. This is in keeping
with statistical discrimination and suggests that firms will seek
to minimize future losses from investing in costly training for a
group of workers expected to have higher turnover.

What other approaches are there?

In the absence of researcher-designed randomized experiments,
economists look for opportunities to exploit natural experiments,

in which forces of nature or policies implemented by governments or businesses create treatment and control groups—essentially mimicking a random assignment experiment. Researchers studying such natural experiments to investigate labor market discrimination examine responses to, for instance, changes in quotas, hiring practices, sex ratios, or pay rules.

One natural experiment on sex discrimination in hiring that received a lot of attention looked at the hiring of musicians into a number of high-profile orchestras. During the 1970s and 1980s, the practice of auditioning musicians for selection into orchestras in many major US cities underwent a dramatic change. Previously, musicians played on the stage in view of the selection committee; however, those chosen for the jobs were often handpicked before the audition by the musical director, and frequently were selected from among the students of a small number of well-connected teachers. In a move to democratize the process and open these coveted positions up to a much wider range of musicians, candidates played behind a screen, completely anonymous to the selection committee, and were thus judged solely on the sound of their performance. The adoption of this blind audition increased the number of female musicians who advanced out of the first round and ultimately increased the proportion of women hired. The masking of candidates' gender was estimated to account for one-quarter to one-third of the increase in female orchestra members—a substantial increase in women in a highly skilled, previously male-dominated occupation.

The major difficulty in this methodology is that the researchers have no control over the exact research question that can be answered. One must be clever in ferreting out a natural experiment that sheds light on questions of labor market discrimination and be lucky enough to have data available to measure changes in the affected labor market outcomes.

7

WHY CAN'T THE GOVERNMENT JUST FIX THE PAY GAP?

A series of legal provisions that have been enacted at the federal level throughout the past six decades address various forms of discrimination, including discrimination on the basis of sex. States have also enacted their own provisions. Unfortunately, legislation alone does not fully confer protection from discrimination. In Chapter 6 we showed the difficulty researchers have understanding if, and identifying when, discrimination has occurred. It is also difficult to prove discrimination in a court of law. In this chapter we discuss the evolution, enforcement, and effectiveness of anti-discrimination policies in the United States. At the end of the chapter, we focus attention on some new approaches to eradicating discrimination. Any policies designed to correct pay distortions associated with discrimination can benefit not just women themselves but the economy as a whole. However, some policies, while well-intentioned, may themselves create inefficiencies.

What are the consequences of discrimination for the economy?

When a group of people is discriminated against, the economy is inadequately remunerating a large group of valuable employees and the market sends a number of misleading signals. First, since pay is a marker for productivity, the most productive workers may not be matched with employment that best uses their skills. Women, for example, might never be considered for occupations in which they might excel. Second, pay discrimination may distort other decisions. For example, women and minority workers, who face pay discrimination, may pursue lower-than-optimal amounts of education. These distortions have a negative impact on the economy, as overall productivity is lower than it could be and labor is misallocated.

The career trajectory of Sandra Day O'Connor, the first woman on the US Supreme Court, provides a stark example. Justice O'Connor graduated from Stanford Law School in 1952 in two years rather than the usual three, was editor of the law review, and ranked third in her class of 102 students. Yet she had difficulty finding a paying job as an attorney because of her gender. She ultimately found employment as a deputy county attorney in San Mateo, California, but only after she offered to work for no salary and without an office—she shared office space with a secretary! O'Connor ultimately served as the attorney general of Arizona and in 1981 rose to the position of Supreme Court justice. There can be no doubt that O'Connor faced gender discrimination. Due to the mismatch between her skills and her jobs and an arguably slower progression than a man might have had, the legal profession and society as a whole missed out on the contributions that she could have made early in her career. This example focused on a woman who ultimately attained a prestigious occupation, but this misallocation of resources is potentially applicable to the more than 75 million women in the labor force who work for lower wages than their male counterparts.

How can we justify the existence of anti-discrimination laws?

From the perspective of economists, there are two justifications for anti-discrimination laws. The first is on the basis of equity.

If women are being treated unfairly, we may rationalize such laws on the grounds that they force employers to treat all labor market participants equally. Why should equally qualified women or minorities be denied access to higher-paying jobs or earn less money for doing equal work? And we should not lose sight of the fact that discrimination affects not only the worker but also their children because family income is reduced. This is an important way that inequality in opportunity is passed down from generation to generation.

The second justification is on the basis of efficiency. One important task of the labor market is to allocate labor across all the possible firms in the economy in an efficient way. How many workers should be employed at one firm and how many at another? This allocation is important because it determines how much we, as a society, can produce. When labor is allocated inefficiently, we end up producing—and consuming—less than we otherwise could. An allocation of workers across firms is said to be efficient when it is impossible to change the current allocation and produce a set of outputs that is more valuable.

What laws protect women from discrimination?

By the early twentieth century, women made up a quarter of the American workforce, but they were paid far less than men, even when they performed the same job. In some states, female workers were also forced to contend with discriminatory laws that restricted their work hours or prohibited them from working at night.

Efforts to remedy this problem escalated during World War II, when thousands of American women entered factory jobs in place of men who had enlisted in the military. In 1942, for example, the National War Labor Board endorsed policies to provide equal pay in instances where women were directly replacing male workers.

In 1945, the US Congress introduced the Women's Equal Pay Act, which would have made it illegal to pay women less than men for work of "comparable quality and quantity." Despite fervent campaigns by women's groups, the measure failed to pass. Little progress was made on pay equity during the 1950s. It was not until 1963 that the United States passed legislation outlawing pay discrimination against women. At that point, women earned only 60 cents for every dollar men earned. In what follows we describe the main laws in place to combat labor market discrimination against women.

What is the Equal Pay Act?

The Equal Pay Act (EPA) was passed in 1963. Former First Lady Eleanor Roosevelt, who at that time was the chair of President Kennedy's Presidential Commission on the Status of Women, along with Representatives Katharine St. George and Edith Green, campaigned passionately for its passage. Despite opposition from business groups such as the Chamber of Commerce and the Retail Merchants Association, Congress passed the EPA as an amendment to the Fair Labor Standards Act of 1938, which originally established the minimum wage and required additional pay for overtime work.

The EPA mandates that employers cannot award unequal wages or benefits to men and women working jobs that require "equal skill, effort, and responsibility, and which are performed under similar working conditions." This law essentially eliminated a common practice of paying women in a firm lower wages than men for doing the same job. The law was less effective than hoped for, however, primarily because men and women did not often do exactly the same work; occupational segregation was widespread in the 1960s.

What is Title VII of the Civil Rights Act?

Title VII of the Civil Rights Act of 1964 made it unlawful for an employer "to refuse to hire or to discharge any individual, or otherwise to discriminate against any individual with respect to his compensation, terms, conditions, or privileges of employment, because of such individual's race, color, religion, sex or national origin." This act is widely regarded as the cornerstone of anti-discrimination legislation in the United States. In 2020, the Supreme Court affirmed that the protections against sex discrimination extended to LGBTQ individuals.

The impetus for Title VII was racial discrimination. In the early 1960s, sex discrimination did not receive the same attention. In fact, the word "sex" was added as an amendment to the proposed Title VII just before the vote took place—by Representative Howard W. Smith of Virginia, a conservative known to oppose all civil rights legislation. One author argues that his action was "a deliberate ploy of foes of the bill to scuttle it."[1] However, there is another interpretation arguing that the addition to the bill was the result of tireless work by women lawmakers and the National Women's Party, whose strategy was to add "sex" to any legislation aimed at expanding or securing rights for any group in hopes of gaining rights for women.[2] Either way, the law passed.

Because "sex" was added to the bill late in the process, the historical record is thin on lawmakers' intention to fight gender discrimination. However, Congress made its intentions to fight gender discrimination very clear with a series of amendments to Title VII, beginning with the Equal Opportunity Act of 1972. This act expanded coverage of Title VII such that nearly all employers were subject to the law, and it established the Equal Employment Opportunity Commission (EEOC) to enforce the provisions of Title VII.

In 1978, Title VII was again amended to specifically protect pregnant women through the Pregnancy Discrimination Act. The law was amended again in 1991 to allow for jury trials in more circumstances and the recovery of compensatory and punitive damages. The 1991 amendment also included the Glass Ceiling Act, which formally recognized that women remained underrepresented in management and other positions with authority in business, and established a Glass Ceiling Commission along with an annual award for promoting a more diverse managerial workforce. In 1995, the Federal Glass Ceiling Commission concluded its work with a report declaring that "today's American labor force is gender and race segregated—white men fill most top management positions in corporations."[3]

Another important amendment to Title VII came in 2009, when President Obama signed the Lilly Ledbetter Fair Pay Act, which established that pay discrimination occurs each time an employee receives a discriminatory paycheck. Lilly Ledbetter was one of the few female supervisors at a Goodyear plant in Gadsden, Alabama, and worked there for close to two decades. When she began her job in 1979, she was paid the same as her male colleagues, but over the years she was awarded smaller raises, and nearly two decades later she found out that she was making 40 percent less than men in comparable positions. Goodyear had a policy that forbade employees to discuss their pay, and Ledbetter only realized that she was the subject of discrimination when she received an anonymous note revealing the salaries of three of the male managers she worked with. Because she found out so much later than the initial discrimination began, the act states that each discriminatory paycheck (rather than the original decision to discriminate) resets the 180-day limit to file a claim.

Lastly, sexual harassment is also covered under Title VII. Unequal power in the workplace has long been a cause of sexual harassment of workers. It was not until 1986 that the Supreme Court recognized sexual harassment as a form of sex discrimination that was covered by Title VII. As noted in Chapter 4, sexual harassment takes two forms—quid pro quo (i.e., an exchange of sexual favors for employment opportunities) and the creation of a hostile work environment (i.e., a work environment that would be intimidating, hostile, or offensive to a reasonable person).

What is affirmative action?

Affirmative action (AA) was established by Executive Order 11246, signed in 1965 by President Johnson to address employment discrimination based on race, color, religion, and national origin. It was not until 1967 that Executive Order 11375 expanded AA to include women, although this was not enforced until the Employment Act of 1972. AA requires every firm with a government contract totaling $50,000 or more to develop an AA employment plan. Many large firms that are not required to do so also voluntarily develop AA plans. AA is not without controversy, and many states have outright banned its use in education and employment settings. Because our focus in this chapter is on employment discrimination, we do not discuss educational AA issues.

What is comparable worth?

Should a truck driver earn more than a social worker, or an engineer more than a librarian? Questions like these are resolved in part by the labor market forces of supply and demand. Advocates of comparable worth argue that occupations dominated by female workers pay less than comparable male-dominated jobs because of systematic discrimination against women. The EPA cannot address these pay differences because women and men rarely do the same work. Under comparable worth, an idea that first received attention in the late 1970s, employers would be required to set wages to reflect the worth of jobs, as determined by evaluation of the job's difficulty, skill level, and other factors and not by market forces. Advocates expect comparable worth to increase pay in jobs dominated by women and to sharply narrow the overall gender gap in wages. Proponents of comparable worth would like to see the EPA reworded to require "equal pay for jobs of equal value."

Putting comparable worth into practice is challenging. How do we determine equal worth? For many years, the federal government, many state governments, and many large corporations have used job evaluation to help determine pay rates, though not necessarily to address gender-based pay differentials.

A job evaluation can take several forms. One of these is the point factor system. First, the nature and tasks of each job in a given organization are described fully. Then the job attributes (called the compensable factors), including skills, effort, responsibility, and the pleasantness of the working conditions, among others, are identified. After these determinations are made, a numerical value is assigned to each compensable factor and evaluators assign weights to each factor according to its importance to the firm. This job evaluation is then used to determine pay. One way to do this is to determine a pay line by plotting the total job points against the pay of the many jobs at each firm, usually with the help of some statistical analysis. The final step is to adjust wages so that jobs with equal points are equally compensated. Researchers typically find that predominantly female jobs are more likely to lie below the pay line than those dominated by men.

An example comes from an application of comparable worth to workers employed by the state of Minnesota, which was an early adopter of comparable worth. Before the application of comparable worth, registered nurses, predominantly women, earned $1,732 per month, while vocational education teachers, predominantly men, were paid $2,260 per month. After the job evaluation, which rated jobs on factors such as required education and training, level of stress, customer contact, and level of responsibility, it was determined that these two occupations were rated the same and so should be compensated the same under comparable worth.

Who enforces these laws and how are they enforced?

In this section, we look at the institutions responsible for enforcing US anti-discrimination laws. All of these enforcement agencies are dependent on government appointments, funding, and staffing, which often results in varying degrees of enforcement from one presidential administration to another.

How are Title VII and the Equal Pay Act enforced?

Enforcement of the EPA and Title VII takes place through the EEOC—an independent, five-member agency appointed by the president with the approval of the Senate. Generally, in order to take action, the EEOC must receive a sworn complaint from an individual, and if the complaint is found to have merit, the EEOC then approaches the offending employer for conciliation. If conciliation is not achieved, the EEOC and the complainant may then go to the court system. The EEOC can also bring class action suits designed to redress discrimination among a group of workers, rather than just one individual at a firm. Class action suits and the possibility of large settlements provide more of a threat to a firm accused of discrimination.

As part of its enforcement efforts, the EEOC requires employers with at least one hundred employees or government contractors with either fifty employees or more than $50,000 in government contracts to submit an EEO-1 Private Sector Report annually. This report is a snapshot of how many racial and ethnic minorities and women are working in a company; the EEOC uses this information to decide which firms should be investigated. Interestingly, the first year that the EEOC was in operation it did not expect to see many sex discrimination lawsuits. After all, the main purpose of Title VII was to eliminate racial discrimination; as we noted earlier, sex was added at the last minute. Yet in the first year, one-third of all charges filed alleged sex discrimination.

Since the passage of Title VII, the courts have wrestled with the question of what is and what is not discrimination as covered by Title VII. The courts use several standards when evaluating claims. The first is "disparate treatment." This applies when individuals are treated differently (paid different wages, offered different promotions) because of their race, sex, color, religion, or national origin and if it can be shown that there was an intent to discriminate. For example, if female applicants are asked to take an employment test but men are not, this is clearly disparate treatment.

Disparate treatment seems like the obvious definition of discrimination. However, the problem with this standard is that a seemingly non-discriminatory hiring practice may have discriminatory outcomes. For example, assume that job applicants for a certain job are required to be over six feet tall; this would obviously lead to far fewer women being hired than men. If it cannot be shown that this requirement is necessary for the job, this hiring rule may create what is called "disparate impact." Under this standard, even if a firm does not intend to discriminate, it can be held liable if its actions lead to discriminatory outcomes. Here the concern is with the result, not the motivation. A hiring policy that appears to be neutral but leads to different impacts by gender (or any of the other protected classes) is prohibited unless the policy can be shown to be necessary for successful job performance.

The threat of a lawsuit and the potential monetary penalties should deter discrimination. However, most lawsuits are resolved without a trial and involve confidential settlements, which may not send a clear, public signal for firms about the potential cost of engaging in discrimination.

How Is Affirmative Action Enforced?

To administer AA, the Office of Federal Contract Compliance Programs (OFCCP) was established. Its job is to conduct a compliance review to investigate and determine whether a firm is engaging in discriminatory practices. This includes close examination of a firm's personnel rosters, payroll figures, and other records as well as employee interviews to determine if the firm has complied with its AA plan. If discrimination is discovered, the OFCCP will recommend corrective action, and in some cases sanctions are imposed.

A firm's AA plan outlines numerical goals, actions, and timetables to increase their employment of women and minorities. The following example illustrates difficulties inherent in implementing AA plans. Suppose a firm believes that it employs too few women as managers. First, the firm must conduct statistical analyses to determine if that is the case. This involves identifying the appropriate pool of applicants from which it should be hiring. Defining the appropriate pool is often difficult, as this discriminating firm may have poisoned the water—if the firm has been known to be unfriendly to women, it is likely that fewer women apply to that firm, and consequently its observed applicant pool will have fewer women than it should. Another option is to define the pool as all female managers in the area. This too is problematic. Perhaps women in the area have not trained for management careers or have left for other areas because of the firm's discrimination.

Even when the firm has identified its labor pool and set its hiring targets, it must then outline actions to meet their goal. To help meet their AA goals, employers often use outreach campaigns, targeted recruitment, employee and management development, and employee support programs. Suppose a firm with 20 percent female managers has set a goal of 40 percent; what should the firm do? One approach is to ensure that 40 percent of its new management hires are female. However, if there is low turnover (i.e. managers are not likely to quit or be fired), using this hiring rule results in slow progress toward the 40 percent goal. The only way to quickly remedy past discrimination may be to disproportionately favor females in hiring. If the firm turns down any better-qualified males to do so, it risks charges of reverse discrimination. Reverse discrimination is said to occur when a less-qualified female or minority group member is hired in place of a more qualified applicant who is not in the protected category (e.g., a white male). Unfortunately, even when members of protected groups are equally qualified, they may be suspected by co-workers of being less qualified if they are thought to be AA hires. While specific quotas are not legal under AA, the policy is often interpreted that way.

How effective are these laws?

Here we examine the efficacy of these major anti-discrimination laws. The EPA and Title VII of the Civil Rights Act were introduced in the early 1960s. Because women's median earnings were 60 percent of men's earnings when these laws were implemented and this pay ratio did not move much in the ensuing decade, critics have argued that these laws did not improve gender pay equality. But, as we know, there was much going on during that time related to women in the labor market, making such a simplistic evaluation of the law suspect. The challenge for researchers lies in how to examine the efficacy of a law that had nearly universal coverage (and hence for which there was no control group) and which was enacted during a time when other social trends, legislation, and litigation were occurring that affected the employment and wage outcomes of women and minorities. Addressing this question relies on the research of economists and other social scientists. In conducting this research, it is important to distinguish the law's actual effect on the gender pay gap from factors that are correlated with the law. Failure to find evidence that these laws improved women's labor market outcomes can mean either that there was little discrimination to correct or that the anti-discrimination law was ineffective. The effectiveness of AA, which came over a decade later, is easier to assess because not all firms are subject to the law, which allows for a comparison of labor market outcomes for employees at firms that are and are not covered by AA.

How effective is the Equal Pay Act?

Many scholars agree that it is unlikely that the EPA had a large impact on the earnings of women. Until recently, women did not often do precisely the same type of work as men did, so consequently this law was unlikely to be effective at eliminating gender pay gaps. It is also challenging for women to bring a successful claim under the EPA because they must establish that the work they and their male colleagues do is equal in required skill, effort, responsibility, and working conditions. However, an employer can still offer additional evidence to justify wage differences based on factors other than sex. In 2014, only 19 percent of the cases brought to the EEOC alleging violations of the EPA were resolved in favor of the women who claimed discrimination. It seems unlikely that the EPA alone, given the difficulty of the burden of proof, will close the gender pay gap.

Prior to the enactment of the EPA, many, but not all, states had their own equal pay laws, which allows a comparison of the earnings and employment situations for women in states with and without such laws. Because some states did not adopt equal pay acts and those that did adopted them at different times, researchers could compare employment and earnings outcomes of women in states that did enact such laws to states that did not, both before and after the laws were enacted. One study that made such comparisons found that because an equal pay constraint raises the relative price of female labor, state equal pay laws for women reduced the relative employment of both Black and white women. This highlights the difficulty inherent in developing anti-discrimination policies—they can inadvertently involve trade-offs and unintended results. In this case the trade-off is between higher wages and lower employment, and the unintended result is that fewer women enjoy a boost in pay.[4]

How effective is Title VII of the Civil Rights Act?

The narrow focus of the EPA did not address discrimination in hiring or promotion. Protection for women was expanded when Title VII of the Civil Rights Act passed. Yet evaluating the efficacy of Title VII faces the same obstacles that arose when evaluating the EPA.

The potential costs associated with non-compliance might provide the best incentive for firms to comply with Title VII, and a number of studies have used this angle to examine its efficacy. Most of these studies, however, did not address sex discrimination. A notable exception is a study that was done in the 1970s that found that the number of Title VII class action suits per corporation within an industry and state was associated with significant improvement in the employment of Black women into professional and managerial occupations.[5]

A more recent analysis focused on 171 lawsuits that occurred between 1997 and 2008. The study sought to understand how Title VII litigation affected the managerial diversity of the companies involved. This statistical analysis isolated the effect of lawsuits on the percentages of white women, Black women, and Black men in management by comparing the numbers in the year before a lawsuit with the subsequent three years, while controlling for other factors that might affect managerial diversity.[6] Overall, results showed, a discrimination lawsuit led to measurable gains in managerial representation for all three groups studied. Nevertheless, the authors note that outcomes were influenced by the amount of media coverage, whether and how policy changes were mandated, and the amount of the payouts.

How effective is affirmative action?

Because not all firms are subject to AA, it has been somewhat easier to ascertain its effectiveness in combating discrimination. However, such analysis is complicated because over time, the intended beneficiaries of such policies, women and minorities, have been increasing their LFPR. Disentangling the part of this increase that is due directly to AA from the part that reflects other policies or underlying trends is challenging.

As noted earlier, because AA is a program that specifically applies to firms that are federal contractors, scholars can compare the employment outcomes of covered groups at firms that are federal contractors (and thus subject to the policy) to firms that are not. Using such a comparison, a comprehensive study of 100,000 large private-sector firms across all industries and regions from 1973 to 2003 concluded that Black and Native American women and men were the main beneficiaries of federally mandated AA programs and that the fastest growth in employment for these groups occurred during the 1970s and early 1980s.[7]

In 1996, the state of California passed Proposition 209, which essentially outlawed existing local and state AA programs in education, public hiring, and contracting, except for those cases where federal law required such programs. The passage of this proposition allowed for a comparison of the employment outcomes for minorities in California before and after AA was removed to the corresponding outcomes for white men. This difference was then compared to the same difference in states not undergoing similar changes in law. As a whole, the results of this study indicated that the overall impact of Proposition 209 was to move women and minorities out of the labor force. This research suggests that the removal of AA in California made it more difficult for women and minorities to find work.[8]

What might the future hold with respect to closing the gender pay gap?

Given that women still only earn just over 80 percent of what men earn, it is clear that the current laws, which have been in place for over fifty years, are not entirely effective at countering gender-based pay discrimination. In what follows we highlight approaches that are under discussion to further reduce the gender wage gap, with an eye toward how they might affect both equity for workers and market efficiency. To understand the relationship between equity and efficiency, recall our discussion of the discrimination faced by the first woman on the Supreme Court and the market distortions and inefficiencies that resulted. As we have seen, discrimination itself leads to inefficiency, and combating it should improve market efficiency. What else is happening to reduce the gap?

What is intersectional discrimination?

An individual's identity can never be reduced to solely one characteristic, such as race, sex, socioeconomic status, religion, sexual orientation, gender identity, ability, or age. Intersectionality is a framework for understanding how these identities overlap with one another and confer disadvantages to some people in the workplace and society. For example, a Black woman may face discrimination based on both her race and her sex.

Unfortunately, the way that Title VII is worded makes it hard to redress the type of bias that Black women (and others facing intersectional discrimination) face in the labor market. Legal scholars have criticized the passage in Title VII that states that discrimination is illegal based on "an individual's race, color, religion, sex or national origin" for its use of the word "or," claiming that it has made it difficult to bring a discrimination claim based on membership in more than one protected class. Intersectionality provides a framework in which those who suffer multiple forms of discrimination can identify each of those forms, instead of pigeonholing their discrimination as, for example, based solely on race or sex.

The theory of intersectionality dates back to legal scholar Kimberlé Williams Crenshaw and her documentation of the way in which Black women were (poorly) served by the legal system in discrimination cases that failed to consider the ways that race and gender intersected in shaping their economic experience and how that experience differed from those of white women and Black men. Some legal scholars call for Title VII to be amended such that it includes the clause "or any combination thereof" to allow plaintiffs to combine two or more protected classes. The EEOC has increasingly recognized the intersectional nature of discrimination, and it seems certain that at least part of the legal landscape of the future with respect to anti-discrimination laws will address intersectionality. Allowing for intersectional discrimination should improve market efficiency as individuals receive the appropriate redress for wage distortions against them.

What is a transparent paycheck?

Paycheck transparency is a policy to force employers to explain and/or close the gender pay gap. Simply put, it is the extent to which employees are familiar with each other's pay levels. Some employers (e.g., state governments) post the pay of their employees publicly. Websites such as Glassdoor and PayScale also encourage anonymous posting of salaries and positions to help others.

The practice is somewhat controversial in the United States. Despite the fact that sharing such information is legal, many employers have policies stating that employees cannot divulge salary information, and many employees do not realize it is perfectly within their rights to discuss their salaries with others.[9] A survey by the Institute for Women's Policy Research revealed that in 2014, about half of all workers reported that the discussion of wage and salary information is either prohibited or discouraged by their employer and could even lead to discipline. In an effort to combat such employer-mandated violations of individual employees' rights, some states have gone so far as to ban employer paycheck secrecy policies. In 2016, President Obama issued an executive order prohibiting many firms contracting with the US government from retaliating against employees for disclosure of compensation information.

Does a policy of paycheck transparency help to close the gender wage gap? If advocates of more open pay discussions are correct, those states that adopted bans on paycheck secrecy should have better wage outcomes for women and a smaller gender wage gap. A study compared the earnings of highly educated women in states that have banned pay secrecy to the earnings of highly educated women working in states without such bans, both before and after the adoption of the laws. The author reported that college-educated women had 3 percent higher earnings and that the gender wage gap was therefore lower after paycheck transparency was adopted.[10]

An advantage of paycheck transparency is that it increases information for market participants—employees and employers alike. One of the central tenets of a market economy is that efficiency is enhanced when information is widely available and costless. This policy moves us in the direction of both improved equity and efficiency.

What is wrong with asking about prior paychecks when hiring?

One firm practice that has been specifically implicated in perpetuating the gender pay gap is asking about prior salary when hiring a new employee. Because women earn less than men, asking about and then matching that salary is likely to continue the cycle of pay disadvantage to women. Because they typically start their careers at lower salaries than their male co-workers, women face an uphill battle trying to level the field. Challenges to this practice are winding their way through the courts as we write this book. Several states have enacted legislation that would ban the practice of asking employees their previous compensation.

Of course, limiting any information sounds antithetical to market efficiency. As noted earlier, however, pay discrimination is itself a costly distortion of market signals, so if relying on prior salaries perpetuates discrimination, eliminating their use can improve efficiency. These laws hold promise for improving pay equity without harming market efficiency, but it will be some time before their effectiveness in reducing the gender pay gap can be measured.

What is the status of comparable worth?

More than twenty US states have implemented some sort of comparable-worth pay scales for their state government jobs. In 1986, the state of Minnesota was among the first to do so. Other countries also make use of comparable worth in setting pay for government workers. In 2018, Iceland introduced the first policy in the world that requires companies and institutions with more than twenty-five employees to prove that they pay men and women equally for a job of equal worth. Starting in 2020, firms were fined if they were not in compliance.

So why has the United States not passed a comparable worth law? While comparable worth is appealing to many, economists and many policymakers express some concerns, not over the end result of fair pay but about the consequences of altering market signals as the means to facilitate gender pay equity. The job evaluation process is, as you may have already thought, highly subjective. Although it makes sense for job attributes such as skills and working conditions to influence pay, there is no single correct method for determining the number of points assigned to each attribute, or for determining the weight each attribute should have in the overall worth of each job. After all, consider which takes the most skill and to what degree: providing care for a group of preschoolers, solving an engineering problem, translating a language, or managing a restaurant? How should skill be weighted relative to working conditions or accountability? Answers to these questions are bound to be subjective. Therefore, different job evaluation systems and different job evaluators are apt to assign different rankings to the same set of occupations, resulting in incomparable worth. That, indeed, has often been the result.

The imposition of comparable worth would likely raise pay in traditionally female jobs. This raises a common policy concern regarding the trade-off between wages and employment. Because the higher pay in female jobs would raise costs, an unintended consequence would be that employers would have an incentive to reduce employment in such jobs, by automating or reducing the scale of operations, for example. Workers with the most skills would be more likely to keep their jobs, while those without the skills or experience to merit the higher pay would be let go. The ironic result is that fewer workers would be employed in traditionally female jobs. Less-skilled women would lose out to more-skilled women and, quite possibly, to men who would be attracted by the higher pay. Whether or not there are large trade-offs between wages and employment from implementing comparable policies is an open question.

What is the Paycheck Fairness Act?

The Paycheck Fairness Act (PFA) is a proposed update to the EPA. It aims to reduce gender pay disparities by making wages more transparent. This would be accomplished by mandating that the Department of Labor assist employers in collecting and disseminating wage-related data. This information would allow reasonable comparisons of wages between employees within clearly defined geographic areas to determine fair wages. This would encourage businesses to adopt comparable-worth-like pay structures.

The PFA would also require employers to prove that wage discrepancies are tied to legitimate business qualifications and not gender. If the firm's practices are upheld, an employee still has recourse if they can demonstrate that there is an alternative employment practice that would serve the same business purpose without producing the gender-based differential. Finally, the PFA would prohibit firms from taking retaliatory action against employees who raise concerns about gender-based wage discrimination.

Although aspects of the PFA lead to the same efficiency concerns as comparable worth, the dissemination of better pay data improves information (and hence efficiency) and the legal recourse allows targeted adjustments to discriminatory pay distortions. Although the PFA was first introduced nationally in 1997 and continues to be reintroduced annually, it has repeatedly failed to gain the congressional votes necessary to pass. However, many states have passed legislation that incorporates some of the provisions of the PFA.

8

HOW DO WOMEN FARE
IN RETIREMENT?

This chapter focuses on issues related to retirement and aging most salient to women and recognizes that, even with the generally high standard of living in the United States, not everyone is afforded the privilege of a comfortable retirement. Although both men and women must prepare for and make the decision when to retire from the workforce, the conditions faced by women differ from those faced by men. Specifically, when men retire they are likely to have a younger, possibly healthier spouse who may still be working. Women, on the other hand, are likely to outlive their husbands. They are more likely to face economic hardship as they age because they need to make their retirement savings last far longer than do men. We know that the gender pay gap accumulates: one estimate suggests that women earn, on average, $850,000 less than men over their lifetimes. Because of these earnings differences, women and men have, on average, starkly different incomes during retirement; both Social Security and employer-provided retirement plans are impacted by earnings. All of these differences contribute to significantly higher poverty rates for older women as compared to men, leading to a number of policy discussions and proposals aimed at addressing financial insecurity in retirement.

How do people decide when to retire?

Retirement looks quite different across the socioeconomic divide. For some who labored in low-paying jobs or who may be unable to continue working as long as needed to secure a comfortable retirement, their savings dissipate rapidly and making ends meet can become a struggle. For those who had more lucrative jobs or were able to save more, retirement may be a time to spend the stockpile of savings that have accrued during their work life—as exemplified by a bumper sticker often displayed on an RV that announces, "We're spending our kid's inheritance" (referring to the owner's travel on an extended road-trip vacation). Although in both scenarios participation in the labor force has ended (or slowed down), the main difference between them is the contrasting financial circumstances.

What exactly does it mean to be retired? There is no single definition of retirement, but most scenarios include at least one of these criteria: the acceptance of a pension and/or Social Security benefits to accompany the voluntary (or sometimes forced) exit from one's career, reductions in work hours and salary, or complete withdrawal from the workforce. What all of these criteria have in common is a reduction in market work and a change in the source(s) and (usually) amounts of income.

A simple financial model of factors that influence the decision to retire goes something like this. People work and save over their lives, and they assess a number of questions: (1) What will their future lifetime earnings be? (2) How much will they need or want to spend and save in the future? (3) How long will they be able or want to work? (4) How long will they live? Implied in this list are more nuanced factors, such as how much interest they will earn on their savings and investments, how much their health care will cost, how much they want to leave to their children or charity, and so on. However, we will focus on the simple model, as it highlights the important points quite clearly.

The forward-looking individual (or couple) will plan to save and invest enough during their work life and adjust their retirement age(s) so that they have enough to support themselves through their expected retirement lifespan(s) and provide for any bequests that they might hope to leave as part of their estate. Other sources of income in addition to savings enter into this equation as well. Any stream of retirement benefits, from the government and/or employer-provided retirement funds, reduces the need for private savings. For individuals who have enjoyed prosperous careers and seen their retirement nest egg grow through regular savings and employer contributions to their retirement accounts, these calculations are often made in consultation with a financial advisor. For those who have not had such prosperous careers, saving for retirement is more difficult and their future economic security may rely primarily on Social Security.

The model leads to a few conclusions. Individuals who anticipate a shorter life expectancy, who expect high rates of return on their investments, and who have generous retirement benefits may choose to retire earlier, but even this is complicated. High-income earners, for example, may be able to save adequately and retire early, but on the other hand, they face a higher opportunity cost (in terms of forgone earnings) when they decide to stop working. Another obvious feature of this model, however, is that there is uncertainty about nearly every aspect: future lifetime earnings and spending needs, life expectancy, and rates of return on investment and savings are unknown, especially early in one's career. This uncertainty helps explain why there are often large differences between retirees in terms of standard of living and inheritances passed on to beneficiaries.[1] There are gender differences in much of this planning. Women tend to underestimate the chances of living long into old age, while men tend to overestimate their chances; women invest their retirement funds in less risky assets, and they have a stronger preference for leaving bequests to their children than do men.

This discussion highlights the financial considerations, but there is more involved in the decision to retire. An individual's enjoyment (or lack thereof) and ability to continue working, the activities that they would pursue if they were not working, and their health all play a role. Just like the decision to work at any age, each individual will weigh the benefits of working (income, eligibility for health insurance, and accrual of additional retirement benefits) against the value of non-market time (leisure activities and time spent caring for relatives, among other activities). The retirement status of a spouse may also play a role in the value of non-market time (one way or the other). Spouses often retire at the same time, which means that women generally retire at younger ages. When the value of non-market time, including the ability to support oneself, exceeds the benefits of working, an individual will choose to retire.

How long is retirement for men and women?

The simple answer is that retirement begins from the time that an individual transitions out of the workforce and continues through the remainder of their life. There are two determinants of the length of time spent in retirement. The first is when an individual leaves the workforce, and the second is how long they live after retirement. Not surprisingly, there are gender differences in the answers to both of these questions.

Although most countries have historically imposed mandatory retirement ages, in the United States today, mandating retirement at a certain age is discrimination under the Age Discrimination and Employment Act of 1967. Although allowing work into old age is typically the case in developed countries, many developing countries still have mandatory retirement ages, and often specify different ages for men and women. In China, for example, the mandatory retirement age has been sixty for men and fifty for women (fifty-five for female government employees, ironically) for more than four decades. With a rapidly aging population, a dramatically shrinking workforce resulting from low fertility since the 1970s, and the exploding financial burden of providing for retired workers, changing these retirement requirements is a hot topic in China—and one not particularly well received by workers. Because China's pension system is designed so that there are no extra benefits for the recipient if they delay retirement, most workers oppose increasing the retirement age.

In the United States, age sixty-five has become synonymous with retirement. This came about quite naturally, as for years sixty-five was the age at which both men and women became eligible for full Social Security benefits and Medicare health benefits. Despite these eligibility criteria, Americans sometimes retire in advance of their eligibility or continue working beyond age sixty-five. Even among those aged seventy-five and above, while 87 percent of men and 93 percent of women report being out of the labor force, the remainder still participate, albeit perhaps just part-time.

The average male worker in the United States retires at age 64.6, and the average female worker retires at age sixty-two.[2] Those two extra years of spending must be accounted for in women's retirement planning. Less-educated workers and those in physically demanding occupations retire at younger ages than more-educated workers in white-collar jobs. In fact, while the age at retirement has held steady or declined for less-educated workers, the retirement age has increased over the last few decades for the most-educated workers.

Life expectancy is the other part of the calculation of time spent in retirement. With today's longevity trends, individuals who retire in their early sixties could spend nearly as much time retired as they spent in their careers—a scenario that is more likely for women than for men. The Social Security Administration provides a life expectancy calculator to aid individuals in planning their retirement. When life expectancy is factored into the equation, gender differences in the estimated time spent in retirement grow substantially larger. As

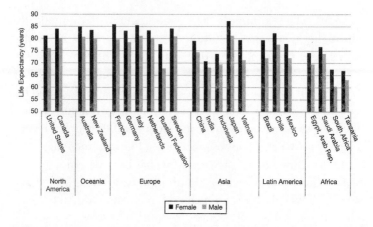

Figure 8.1 Life Expectancy at Birth by Gender for Selected Countries
Source: 2015–2020 United Nations.

has been true for centuries and across all countries, women experience lower mortality at every age and have longer life expectancy than men. Figure 8.1 shows life expectancy at birth for men and women in selected countries and illustrates that in all cases, women live longer than men. For example, the life expectancy for men in the United States is 76.3 years, while women are expected to live to the age of 81.3. The average gender difference in life expectancy across these twenty-two countries is five years. The largest difference is in Russia, where male life expectancy is more than ten years lower than that of women. The life expectancy advantage for women is smallest in India and Saudi Arabia.

In the United States there are also differences in life expectancy by race and ethnicity, as shown in Figure 8.2. White non-Hispanic women and men have a life expectancy at birth of 81.1 and 76.2 years of age, respectively—a gap of nearly five years. This is in contrast to much lower life expectancy for Black women (78.0 years) and men (71.3 years). In what has long been referred to as the "Hispanic paradox," the life expectancy of Hispanic women (84.3 years) and men (79.1 years)

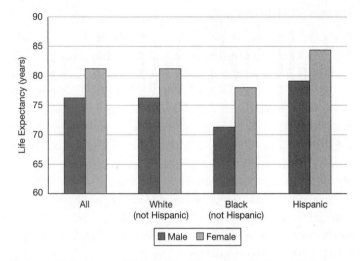

Figure 8.2 Life Expectancy at Birth in the United States by Race/Ethnicity and Gender
Source: CDC 2019.

exceeds that of non-Hispanic white women and men.[3] The bottom line is that for women of all races and ethnicities, greater female longevity combined with an earlier retirement age means that, on average, women spend eight or nine years longer than men in retirement. Additionally, women typically are married to a man two years their senior. Since women out-live men, married men spend their retirement years with a younger, often healthier wife by their side. Married women are likely to spend some time (seven years on average) as widows at the end of their lives.

Where does retirement income come from?

Individuals in the United States typically get their retirement income from two sources. The government has long provided support for older workers through the Social Security system, but increasingly, retirees are also benefiting from retirement plans provided through their employers.

How does Social Security work?

The Social Security Act was signed into law in 1935 to ensure that the elderly and the disabled had financial security. Social Security is financed through a payroll tax—12.2 percent of a worker's earnings are paid into the Social Security system each year up to a maximum level of earnings, which is adjusted annually (in 2021 this maximum was $142,800).[4] The employee and the employer contribute equally to the payroll tax. Social Security payments are sent to beneficiaries monthly and are adjusted annually for cost-of-living changes.

To receive Social Security benefits based upon their own earnings record, individuals must have worked for forty quarters (ten years) and reached a certain threshold level of pay during each of those quarters. The amount of the monthly Social Security benefit depends on the number of years that an individual worked and how much they earned annually. Although an individual is eligible to collect Social Security at age sixty-two, full benefits are not available until an individual reaches full retirement age (FRA). For decades, the FRA was age sixty-five, but concerns over the solvency of the Social Security system as fertility rates have fallen and as the baby boom generation begins to retire have led to increases in the FRA. These increases are currently being phased in and depend on one's year of birth—for those born in 1960 or later, the FRA is sixty-seven years. Delaying the collection of benefits beyond the FRA further increases the amount of the benefit received; an individual who delays collecting until age seventy (the age of eligibility for maximum benefits) will have a higher monthly Social Security payment than they would have received had they started collecting benefits earlier, at age sixty-seven. Individuals can work while collecting benefits, and many do, at least for a few years. There are rules around how much can be earned while collecting Social Security benefits—the Social Security Administration provides more detailed information on this topic.

The Social Security system is structured such that working individuals pay the Social Security tax, but families receive the benefits.[5] When a single woman works and pays Social Security payroll taxes for ten years, she is eligible to collect benefits based on her own earnings. When a married woman works and pays into Social Security for at least ten years, she is also eligible to collect benefits based on her own earnings, but if she chooses, she can instead receive up to 50 percent of her husband's benefit (i.e., a spousal benefit), although she cannot collect both. Because men tend to work longer and earn more, some married women are eligible for a larger benefit based on their husband's earnings record than on their own.

Married women who did not work outside of the home have a number of options for collecting Social Security. For example, in addition to the husband's receipt of his full benefits, the wife is also eligible for half of her husband's Social Security benefit even though only the husband paid payroll taxes. Widows can receive 100 percent of their spouse's Social Security benefit as long as they have reached FRA. Finally, divorced women are entitled to collect 50 percent of their ex-husband's benefits if he is receiving Social Security or is deceased, as long as she has reached FRA, the marriage lasted at least ten years, and she is currently unmarried.

In the case of a two-earner family, Social Security becomes more complicated. In the case when a wife earned substantially less than her husband and/or only worked for a few years, the couple will receive 150 percent of his benefits—assuming her earnings were low enough that she is better off collecting as his spouse. Thus, they get the same benefits they would have had if the wife did not work at all, even though they both paid into the system. In the case where the wife has worked continuously for relatively high earnings and the husband has as well, they will likely receive higher benefits collecting on their own earnings as compared to the family where the wife did not work at all.

The type of family that benefits most from the current structure of the Social Security system is the traditional one, where the husband worked in the formal labor market and the wife specialized in unpaid household work. In this case, only the husband pays into Social Security through the payroll tax, and upon his retirement the family receives 150 percent of his benefits. This was the most common family structure when Social Security first began, which in part explains this payment system. Tax experts have noted that when it comes to Social Security, wives who work in the formal labor market essentially subsidize those who do not. Despite these accommodations for married women, the Social Security Administration reported in 2020 that the average woman's Social Security benefit was 80 percent of the average man's in 2019.[6]

Because Black women are more likely to be single and when married are more likely to be equal earners with their husbands, they tend not to collect the spousal benefits that were designed to provide for non-working wives.

Despite being designed for a traditional family structure, which is becoming increasingly less common, Social Security remains an important component of income for many older women.

How Do employer-sponsored retirement plans work?

Retirement plans through an employer are another primary source of income for US retirees. An individual's employer-provided retirement plan may take one of two forms: a defined-benefit plan or a defined-contribution plan. A defined-benefit plan means that payments are made into a pension fund throughout the employee's work life, and after employment for a prescribed period of time (called vesting), upon retirement the employee becomes entitled to receive monthly benefits from this fund. The formula that determines the monthly retirement benefit typically includes the number of years worked in covered employment, the employee's prior salary, and the employee's age. Note that this list does not include gender. There is little to no risk to the retiree that this gender-neutral monthly retirement income changes, and it continues throughout the retiree's life regardless of longevity. These traditional defined-benefit pension plans are required by law to offer spousal survivor benefits (which require the consent of both partners to be waived) and so confer retirement benefits to married partners who may have specialized in home production or worked in less lucrative occupations.[7]

Defined-contribution plans, on the other hand, are set up so that regular contributions—typically a percentage of income deducted from the employee's paycheck and an additional percentage of income provided as a benefit from the employer—are made on behalf of each employee. These funds accrue to the employee's retirement plan, usually a 401(k), and the employee has the ability to select the types of assets that make up their retirement account, considering associated risk and expected return. In the case of defined-contribution retirement plans, decisions about the degree of risk of the investments are made by the individual employee. Under these plans, after a number of years of employment, and often after a required age, the employee is entitled to the full value of the account, to be used to provide income after retirement.[8] Should the account's value not be fully used during the retiree's lifetime, the remainder becomes part of the employee's estate and can be bequeathed to relatives or charities as the donor sees fit. But the other possibility inherent in this type of retirement plan is the risk that the account will not provide sufficient income to last for the remainder of the retiree's life.

There are a number of reasons men and women fare differently under defined-benefit or defined-contribution plans. Monthly payments from defined-benefit plans are not explicitly adjusted for gender; they are usually calculated as a percentage of earnings while working (or a percentage of the most recent or highest-earning years). Less time in the labor force and lower salaries for women translate into fewer and smaller contributions into defined-contribution plans and a correspondingly smaller account balance at the time of retirement. In fact, according to a 2019 analysis of defined-contribution plans by Vanguard, the median balance in women's retirement funds was only 65 percent of the median balance in men's accounts.[9] It follows, then, that—given the likelihood that they will spend more years of life post-retirement—a defined-benefit plan that provides continuous payments regardless of longevity is more beneficial for women than for men. However, the lower cost of administration for employers and the shifting of the risk of low investment returns to the employee has resulted in defined-contribution plans becoming increasingly more common. There remain some occupations that continue to offer defined-benefit plans, particularly those in which union representation is high. These include female-dominated industries such as state and local government, teaching, and nursing, as well as male-dominated industries such as protective services (policing and firefighting), utilities, and transportation.

How much income do people have when they retire? How does this vary by gender and race/ethnicity?

How much income people have in retirement naturally depends on how much they worked, their earnings, their marital status, what type of retirement plan they have, and how much they were able to save. For example, the presence of a gender wage gap means that women's Social Security benefits, if they collect on their own earnings, will on average be smaller than men's. And since women are more likely to work part-time, they are less likely to have a pension or 401(k) plan at all. Only one-third of part-time employers offer retirement plans to their workers.

Figure 8.2 shows the sources of retirement income by gender, age, and race/ethnicity. The height of each bar is the total income from all sources for each group. As is typical, white men in both age groups have by far the highest incomes. Hispanic women in both age groups have the lowest incomes. Within each race/ethnic and age group, men have more total income than do women. Only white men have average total income exceeding $60,000. In the older age groups, only white and Asian men have total incomes in excess of $30,000 annually. Asian and Hispanic females fare particularly badly as they age, with average annual incomes of less than $20,000.

Figure 8.3 also makes clear that women rely more heavily on Social Security income than do men—a greater proportion of women's income comes from Social Security than does men's for both age groups. This is particularly true for Black and Hispanic women. Between the ages of sixty-five and seventy-four, fully 40 percent of these women's total annual income is from Social Security; when they are aged seventy-five and over, this percentage rises to nearly 60. Social Security is an important part of women's retirement income because, within race at older ages, women on average have a smaller portion of their total income received from an employer-provided retirement plan. Asset income (earnings from savings and investments) falls as people age because they spend down their assets. Still, asset income is twice as high for white men as compared to all other groups.

Although we think of these age groups as representing the retired population, people choose their own retirement timing, and so not everyone in these age groups has ceased working. Figure 8.3 shows that labor market earnings make up a substantial portion of income for both men and women aged sixty-five to seventy-four, while earnings drop off substantially for those aged seventy-five and older. The presence of earnings even for the oldest individuals reflects the fact that some people have not fully retired by age seventy-five.

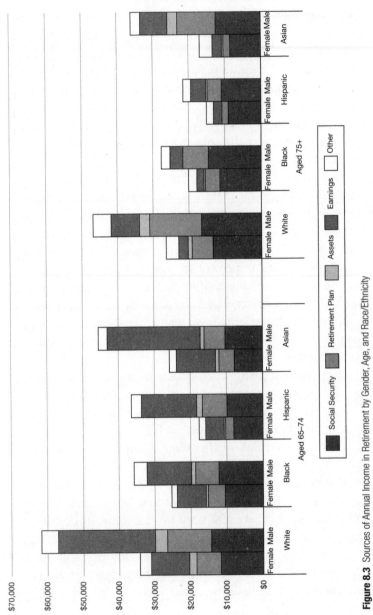

Figure 8.3 Sources of Annual Income in Retirement by Gender, Age, and Race/Ethnicity

Source: 2018 Current Population Survey Annual Social and Economic Supplement. Individuals of other races not shown due to small sample sizes.

Are women destined to be poor as they age?

We've shown that women earn less, are more likely to work part-time, and are more reliant on Social Security in retirement than men. Does this translate into higher poverty rates for older women? Currently the poverty rate for individuals aged sixty-five and over is around 9 percent. Estimates indicate that it would be closer to 40 percent for this group if not for Social Security (the rate would be closer to 50 percent for Black and Hispanic individuals in this age group). Yet, this overall rate masks important gender differences: men aged sixty-five and over have a poverty rate of 7.3 percent, while for similarly aged women the poverty rate is 10.4 percent—30 percent higher. However, scholars note that these gender differences are tied to specific factors such as widowhood and/or disability and are not a product of aging per se. For example, women over the age of seventy-five who are below the poverty line are 18 percent more likely to report disability than similarly aged men below the poverty line. In keeping with what we know about gender differences in mortality, 62 percent of women in poverty over the age of seventy-five are widowed, compared to only 26 percent of men.

Figure 8.4 shows poverty rates disaggregated by gender and race/ethnicity for two age groups: sixty-five to seventy-four years, and seventy-five and above. Recall that we showed that many in the younger age group still have labor market earnings, which partly explains the lower poverty rate for this age group.

Poverty rates increase by age for all racial/ethnic groups except for Asian men, who see a slight decline in poverty as they age. The increase in poverty due to age is markedly larger for women, many of whom are widows. The strikingly high poverty rates for this older group of women can also be attributed to the fact that women live longer, potentially outliving their retirement funds. In the oldest age group, 32 percent of women and 26 percent of men are over the age of eighty.

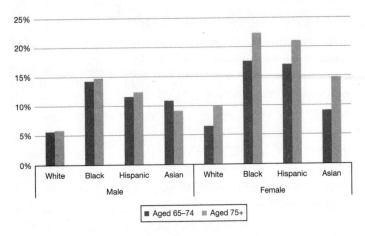

Figure 8.4 Poverty Rates by Gender, Age, and Race/Ethnicity

Source: 2018 Current Population Survey Annual Social and Economic Supplement. Individuals of other races not shown due to small sample sizes.

Between the ages of sixty-five and seventy-four, white men and women experience relatively low poverty rates. But despite the fact that policymakers often use this fact to claim victory over poverty for the elderly, other racial and ethnic groups have not fared nearly as well as whites. Black and Hispanic men and women have the highest poverty rates for both age groups, well above the national average and more than twice the poverty rate for white men. Poverty rates are startlingly high for older women of color. Nearly one in five Black and Hispanic women aged seventy-five or older live in poverty. Although not shown here, estimates indicate that poverty is more common for older women in same-sex couples, compared to those in opposite-sex couples.

How do single women fare later in life?

A woman's current marital status and marital history impact her financial path into retirement. More than half of women between the ages of sixty-five and seventy-four begin retirement while married. Twenty percent were previously married but are divorced or separated, and 18 percent are widowed by the time they are in this age range. The remaining 7 percent of these women had never married.

Having a partner, and particularly a male partner, provides additional financial security later in life. As described earlier, married women, having been part of a couple that (jointly) made decisions about family and financial contributions, can collect spousal benefits from both Social Security and defined-benefit pension plans.[10] Survivor benefits are available to widows and even to some divorced or separated women. These spousal options have been important for generations of women who may have primarily specialized in unpaid household work. Obviously, no such benefits are available to never-married women, who must rely solely on their own Social Security and any employer-provided retirement plans.

For women who have never married and thus lack the option of collecting retirement based on the earnings of a spouse, their own Social Security benefits constitute their primary asset in retirement. Another asset many have is owning a home.[11] If the home is paid off, as is often the case in this age group, homeownership means both that an individual has lower out-of-pocket living expenses and that the home can provide easier means to secure a loan or can be sold if money is needed. Yet without a partner's earnings to cover expenses and save for a home in earlier years, comparatively few single women retirees are homeowners. The difference in homeownership by marital status is pronounced among women of retirement age—among women aged sixty-five to seventy-four, 90 percent of married women own their own home, compared with only 59 percent of never-married women. The difference is even more pronounced for the oldest women: just 50 percent of never-married women aged seventy-five and older are homeowners.

Older, never-married women are at a financial disadvantage because they lack access to a partner's retirement income and

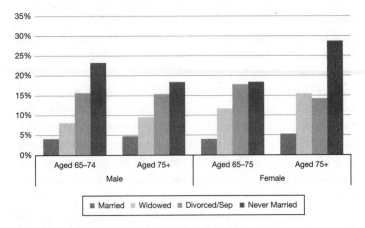

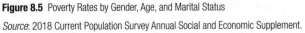

Figure 8.5 Poverty Rates by Gender, Age, and Marital Status

Source: 2018 Current Population Survey Annual Social and Economic Supplement.

have lower rates of homeownership. Figure 8.5 illustrates that the poverty rate for the elderly varies dramatically by marital status. In both age groups shown, married men and women have far lower poverty rates (under 6 percent) compared to those who have never married or were previously partnered. Widowers face poverty rates at or near the national average for this age group. However, poverty rates rise with age for widows, of whom over 15 percent aged seventy-five and older live below the poverty line. The poverty rates for divorced or separated men and women exceed 15 percent across both age groups, but it is the poverty rate for the oldest, never-married women that is the most striking. Nearly 30 percent of never-married women over the age of seventy-five live in poverty.

What options have been suggested to increase retirement security for women?

Many US women face financial insecurity in retirement. Progress in achieving gender pay equity throughout their work lives is an essential starting point to putting women on equal footing when it comes to Social Security benefits, income from employer-provided retirement plans, and retirement savings. Features of retirement plans add to the retirement income disadvantage that women face. For example, a decreasing share of employers offer defined-benefit plans because of high administrative costs coupled with risks to employers of low returns. This switch to 401(k) plans means that employees increasingly bear the risks inherent in unpredictable stock market returns, and under these plans spousal survivors are not necessarily entitled to ongoing benefits. In addition, Social Security, which has emerged as the safety-net retirement plan for American workers and especially for women, clearly is not providing adequately for women in old age. This section highlights some of the policy changes that have been discussed by lawmakers and researchers to improve income security in old age.

How could modifying Social Security help women?

Modify the schedule of Social Security benefits

A suggested modification would allow married couples to select an adjusted schedule of Social Security benefits that would reduce payments while both spouses are alive but limit the drop in benefits after one spouse dies. Because it is typically men who die first, this modification has the potential to reduce poverty rates for elderly widows. An additional possible change would be to increase benefits when recipients reach age eighty-five. This would help older individuals (mainly women) keep up with increases in the cost of living during an exceptionally long, perhaps unplanned, retirement duration.

Caregiver credits

Work credit toward Social Security would be provided to individuals for time spent out of the workforce while caring for dependent children and sick or elderly relatives. The primary objective of these credits, used in almost all public retirement systems in the European Union, would be to improve the adequacy of retirement benefits for women whose gaps in workforce participation typically lead to lower Social Security benefits.[12] Estimates indicate that mothers who collect Social Security benefits on only their own earnings histories receive significantly lower Social Security income.[13]

Social Security as a source of long-term care insurance

The Social Security system could be used to fund a form of long-term care insurance. This would allow new Social Security recipients to elect lower payments when they are younger in exchange for supplementary income in the event of later-life disability. Because the poverty rates for elderly women are often due to disability, this would be particularly effective for that group.

How could changes in employer-based retirement plans help women?

Extend pension coverage to part-time workers

Employers have typically excluded part-time employees from coverage in their defined-contribution retirement plans, but that has recently changed. The passage of the SECURE Act in 2019 requires employers to allow contributions from longtime part-time workers into their 401(k) and other defined-contribution plans beginning in 2024.

Vesting credit for leave time

Because access to employer-provided retirement plans typically requires a vesting period (working for the firm for a designated length of time), it has been suggested that workers who take time off under the Family and Medical Leave Act be allowed to count that time toward meeting a firm's vesting requirements.

Reform employer-based retirement plans

More comprehensive reforms to employer-based retirement plans could provide assistance for women who are less investment-savvy and tend to prefer less-risky investment options. To address these concerns, employer-based retirement plans should provide professional asset management and consulting. It has even been suggested that the funds in defined-contribution plans be invested collectively to allow for increased diversification of risk as in defined-benefit plans.

What other changes could help women in retirement?

An obvious way to improve the economic circumstances of older women compared to men would be to close the gender pay gap throughout their work lives. While many laws aim to do just that, most notably the 1963 Equal Pay Act and Title VII of the 1964 Civil Rights Act, women still face significant shortfalls of income in retirement compared to men. Several policies options are discussed in this section.

Extending work lives into older ages

Another straightforward way to address income shortfalls in retirement is to have people work longer. Women often retire at the same time as their spouse, who is typically a few years older. Since women tend to live longer than their spouses, this disadvantages them economically in their old age. One calculation indicates that if women worked until age seventy, they would receive lifetime benefits equivalent to those of men.

Adding intersectionality to Title VII

Sometimes individuals retire partially—taking a part-time or less-demanding job as compared to their career occupation. Job hunting, particularly as an older woman, is a daunting task given ageist and sexist stereotypes—a specific example of intersectional discrimination, as discussed in Chapter 7. Audit-pair studies report significant age discrimination against older women and underscore the need for modifications to the interpretation of Title VII to allow an intersectional approach (e.g., sex plus age, or sex plus age plus race/ethnicity) in order to effectively address this type of discrimination.

Broaden the existing saver's credit

Although only a small number of taxpayers use it, the "saver's credit" currently provides a federal income tax credit for low-income workers based on the amount they save for retirement. Currently the credit is not refundable, and so it does not provide savings incentives to workers who do not owe income taxes—common among low-income workers. In addition, the amount of the credit decreases on a sliding scale beginning at incomes around $20,000 per year, depending on filing status. Allowing the saver's credit to be refundable, increasing the income limits, and creating campaigns to increase public awareness of this credit can encourage the lowest-wage women (and men) to save for their retirement.

Government provision of defined-contribution retirement plans

Many people, particularly part-time workers and those who work for small firms (who are disproportionately women), do not have access to retirement plans through their workplaces. A number of states are currently working to fill this gap by allowing private individuals to establish retirement accounts by making contributions to the defined-contribution plans already in place for state employees. This provides a low-cost, professionally managed investment option to workers without employer-provided plans.

NOTES

Chapter 1

1. All historical numbers come from the 1900 Decennial Census and are published in table VI, which is available here: https://www2.census.gov/library/publications/1949/compendia/hist_stats_1789-1945/hist_stats_1789-1945-chD.pdf.

2. Leah Platt Boustan and William J. Collins, "The origin and persistence of black-white differences in women's labor force participation," in *Human Capital and History: The American Record*, edited by Leah Platt Boustan, Carola Frydman, and Robert A. Margo, 205–240 (Chicago: University of Chicago Press, 2014).

3. Claudia Goldin, "Female labor force participation: The origin of black and white differences, 1870 and 1880," *Journal of Economic History* 37, no. 1 (1977): 87–108.

4. Claudia Goldin, "The quiet revolution that transformed women's employment, education, and family," *American Economic Review* 96, no. 2 (2006): 1. She was only the third female president of the AEA, and her remarks were addressed to a largely male audience.

5. Eileen Appelbaum, Heather Boushey, and John Schmitt, "The economic importance of women's rising hours of work," Center for American Progress and the Center for Economic and Policy Research, 2014.

6. The OECD promotes economic development and cooperation among its thirty-six member countries, most of which are developed countries, but a few of which are not (e.g., Mexico is an OECD country). Happily for researchers, the OECD maintains

a comprehensive database on labor force and other outcomes. OECD data come up in many places in this book.

7. ATUS is a federally administered survey that collects information on how, where, and with whom Americans spend their time. It started in 2003, is carried out annually, and provides data on a wide range of activities outside of work, including childcare, shopping, and household work.

8. This database, affectionately known as FRED by economists, is maintained at the St. Louis Federal Reserve Bank and is easily accessible to the general public.

9. J. Steven Landefeld, Barbara M. Fraumeni, and Cindy M. Vojtech, "Accounting for household production: A prototype satellite account using the American Time Use Survey," *Review of Income and Wealth* 55, no. 2 (2009): 205–225.

10. V. Miranda, "Cooking, caring and volunteering: Unpaid work around the world," Social, Employment and Migration Working Paper no. 116, OECD, 2011, https://doi.org/10.1787/5kghrjm8s 142-en.

11. Council of Economic Advisors, "The economics of family friendly workplace policies," chapter 4 in Economic Report of the President, Executive Office of the President, Washington, DC, 2015

12. We base our methodology off that used by the Center for American Progress, https://www.americanprogress.org/issues/economy/news/2017/03/07/427556/a-day-in-the-u-s-economy-without-women/.

13. The Human Development Index (HDI) is a way of comparing countries across three dimensions: health, education, and income. Health is gauged by life expectancy at birth; education is measured as a combination of mean years of schooling for adults aged twenty-five years and expected years of schooling for children of school-entering age; income is measured by gross national income per capita.

14. Data for these numbers are from International Labour Stat, www.ilo.org/ilostat, and Verick Sher, "Female labor force participation and development," IZA World of Labor, 2018, https://wol.iza.org/articles/female-labor-force-participation-and-development.

15. Seema Jayachandran, "The roots of gender inequality in developing countries," National Bureau of Economic Research working paper no. 20380, 2014.

16. Jonathan Woetzel et al., "The power of parity: How advancing women's equality can add $12 trillion to global growth," McKinsey Global Institute report no. 7570, 2015.

17. See "A guide to womenomics: The future of the world economy lies increasingly in female hands," *Economist*, April 15 (2006), http://www.economist.com/node/6802551 as an example in the popular press.

18. Data for these ACS calculations can be accessed here: https://www.census.gov/programs-surveys/acs.

19. Shelly J. Lundberg, Robert A. Pollak, and Terence J. Wales, "Do husbands and wives pool their resources? Evidence from the United Kingdom child benefit," *Journal of Human Resources* 32, no. 3 (1997): 463–480, and J. Ward-Batts, "Out of the wallet and into the purse using micro data to test income pooling," *Journal of Human Resources* 43, no. 2 (2008): 325–351.

20. Ian Ayres and Peter Siegelman, "Race and gender discrimination in bargaining for a new car," *American Economic Review* 85 (1995): 304–321.

21. Bill De Blasio and Julie Menin, "From cradle to cane: The cost of being a female consumer. A study of gender pricing in New York City," New York City Department of Consumer Affairs, 2015, https://www1.nyc.gov/assets/dca/downloads/pdf/partners/Study-of-Gender-Pricing-in-NYC.pdf.

22. Authors' calculation from estimates in "Civil rights. Gender discrimination. California prohibits gender-based pricing. Cal. Civ. Code § 51.6 (West Supp. 1996)," *Harvard Law Review* 109, no. 7 (1996): 1839–1844, using the Consumer Price Index.

Chapter 2

1. Ester Boserup, *Woman's Role in Economic Development* (New York: Earthscan, 2007).

2. Alberto Alesina, Paola Giuliano, and Nathan Nunn, "On the origins of gender roles: Women and the plough," *Quarterly Journal of Economics* 128, no. 2 (2013): 469–530.

3. Pauline Grosjean and Rose Khattar, "It's raining men! Hallelujah? The long-run consequences of male-biased sex ratios," *Review of Economic Studies* 86, no. 2 (2019): 723–754.

4. Mireia Borrell-Porta, Joan Costa-Font, and Julia Philipp, "The 'mighty girl' effect: Does parenting daughters alter attitudes towards gender norms?," *Oxford Economic Papers* 71, no. 1 (2019): 25–46.

5. Ebonya L. Washington, "Female socialization: How daughters affect their legislator fathers," *American Economic Review* 98, no. 1 (2008): 311–332.

6. Heidi Gottfried, "The puzzle of gender segregation: From historical roots to contemporary revisions," chapter 3 in *Gender, Work, and Economy: Unpacking the Global Economy* (Cambridge: Polity Press, 2013), 49.

7. See data compiled by the American Economic Association Committee for the Status of Women in the Economics Profession, https://www.aeaweb.org/about-aea/committees/cswep/survey.

8. Claudia Goldin, "The quiet revolution that transformed women's employment, education, and family." *American Economic Review* 96, no. 2 (2006): 1–21.

9. Ariane Hegewisch and Heidi Hartmann, "Occupational segregation and the gender wage gap: A job half done," Institute for Women's Policy Research, January 2016.

10. Patricia Cortes and Jessica Pan, "Occupation and gender," in *Oxford Handbook of Women and the Economy*, edited by Susan L. Averett, Laura M. Argys, and Saul D. Hoffman (New York: Oxford University Press, 2018): 425–452.

11. Philip N. Cohen, "The persistence of workplace gender segregation in the US," *Sociology Compass* 7, no. 11 (2013): 889–899.

12. John H. Pryor, Sylvia Hurtado, Victor B. Saenz, José Luis Santos, and William S. Korn, "The American freshman: Forty year trends," Higher Education Research Institute, University of California, Los Angeles, 2007, https://heri.ucla.edu/PDFs/40T rendsManuscript.pdf.

13. Claudia D. Goldin, "The role of World War II in the rise of women's employment," *American Economic Review* 81, no. 4 (1991): 741–756.

14. Claudia Goldin and Claudia Olivetti, "Shocking labor supply: A reassessment of the role of World War II on women's labor supply," *American Economic Review* 103, no. 3 (2013): 257–262.

15. Caitlin K. Myers, "The power of abortion policy: Reexamining the effects of young women's access to reproductive control," *Journal of Political Economy* 125, no. 6 (2017): 2178–2224.

Chapter 3

1. Cynthia Hess, Tanima Ahmed, and Jeff Hayes, "Providing unpaid household and care work in the United

States: Uncovering inequality," *Institute for Women's Policy Research report #C487*, https://iwpr.org/wp-content/uploads/2020/01/IWPR-Providing-Unpaid-Household-and-Care-Work-in-the-United-States-Uncovering-Inequality.pdf.

2. These data are from the OECD, whose definition is slightly different from the Institute for Women's Policy Research definition in Figure 3.1. Here, time spent in unpaid work includes housework, shopping, care for household members, care for non-household members, volunteering, travel related to household activities, and other unpaid activities.

3. Two seminal articles are Marjorie B. McElroy and Mary Jean Horney, "Nash-bargained household decisions: Toward a generalization of the theory of demand," *International Economic Review* 22, no. 2 (1981): 333–349, and Marilyn Manser and Murray Brown, "Marriage and household decision-making: A bargaining analysis," *International Economic Review* 21, no. 1 (1980): 31–44.

4. Shelly J. Lundberg, Robert A. Pollak, and Terence J. Wales, "Do husbands and wives pool their resources? Evidence from the United Kingdom child benefit," *Journal of Human Resources* 32, no. 3 (1997): 463–480. This is a frequently cited study of the differential impact of income to women and men within a household, and ongoing research has followed up by continuing to examine the impact of this UK transfer (e.g., Julie L. Hotchkiss, "Do husbands and wives pool their resources? Further evidence," *Journal of Human Resources* 40, no. 2 (2005): 519–531, and Jennifer Ward-Batts, "Out of the wallet and into the purse: Using micro data to test income pooling," *Journal of Human Resources* 43, no. 2 [2008]: 325–351).

5. Anna Aizer, "The gender wage gap and domestic violence," *American Economic Review* 100, no. 4 (2010): 1847–1859.

6. Lena Edlund, Hongbin Li, Junjian Yi, and Junsen Zhang, "Sex ratios and crime: Evidence from China," *Review of Economics and Statistics* 95, no. 5 (2013): 1520–1534.

7. Michael E. Martell and Leanne Roncolato, "The homosexual lifestyle: Time use in same-sex households," *Journal of Demographic Economics* 82, no. 4 (2016): 365–398.

8. Charlotte J. Patterson, Erin L. Sutfin, and Megan Fulcher, "Division of labor among lesbian and heterosexual parenting couples: Correlates of specialized versus shared patterns," *Journal of Adult Development* 11, no. 3 (2004): 179–189.

9. Samantha L. Tornello, Bettina N. Sonnenberg, and Charlotte J. Patterson, "Division of labor among gay fathers: Associations with parent, couple, and child adjustment," *Psychology of Sexual Orientation and Gender Diversity* 2, no. 4 (2015): 365–375.

10. Samantha L. Tornello, "Division of labor among transgender and gender non-binary parents: Association with individual, couple, and children's behavioral outcomes," *Frontiers in Psychology* 11 (2020): 15.

11. Statistics are from various published tables from the US Census: https://www.census.gov/data/tables/time-series/demo/same-sex-couples/ssc-house-characteristics.html.

12. Mary Eschelbach Hansen, Michael E. Martell, and Leanne Roncolato, "A labor of love: The impact of same-sex marriage on labor supply," *Review of Economics of the Household* 18 (2020): 1–19.

13. Valerie A. Ramey and Neville Francis, "A century of work and leisure," *American Economic Journal: Macroeconomics* 1, no. 2 (2009): 189–224.

14. As quoted in Jeremy Greenwood, Ananth Seshadri, and Mehmet Yorukoglu, "Engines of liberation," *Review of Economic Studies* 72, no. 1 (2005): 109.

15. Jeremy Greenwood, Ananth Seshadri, and Mehmet Yorukoglu, "Engines of liberation."

16. Many thanks to our partners, who were important contributors to childrearing and made work adjustments themselves.

17. Bureau of Labor Statistics, Employment Characteristics of Families, https://www.bls.gov/news.release/pdf/famee.pdf, last accessed January 27, 2021.

18. Kim Parker, Juliana Menasce Horowitz, Nikki Graff, and Gretchen Livingston, "An inside look at family and medical leave in America," *Pew Research Center, Social and Demographic Trends Project*, May 30, 2020, https://www.pewsocialtrends.org/2017/03/23/an-inside-look-at-family-and-medical-leave-in-america-the-experiences-of-those-who-took-leave-and-those-who-needed-or-wanted-to-but-couldnt/.

19. Rui Huang and Muzhe Yang, "Paid maternity leave and breastfeeding practice before and after California's implementation of the nation's first paid family leave program," *Economics and Human Biology* 16 (2015): 45–59.

20. Rita Hamad, Sepideh Modrek, and Justin S. White, "Paid family leave effects on breastfeeding: A quasi-experimental study

of US policies," *American Journal of Public Health* 109, no. 1
(2019): 164–166.

Chapter 4

1. Pew Research Center, "Women and leadership: Public says
women are equally qualified, but barriers persist," January 15,
2015, https://www.pewresearch.org/wp-content/uploads/
sites/3/2015/01/2015-01-14_women-and-leadership.pdf.
2. Friederike Mengel, "Gender differences in networking," *Economic
Journal* 130, no. 630 (2020): 1842–1873.
3. Zoë B. Cullen and Ricardo Perez-Truglia, "The old boys'
club: Schmoozing and the gender gap," working paper no. 26530,
National Bureau of Economic Research, 2019.
4. Donna K. Ginther, Janet M. Currie, Francine D. Blau, and Rachel
T. A. Croson, "Can mentoring help female assistant professors in
economics? An evaluation by randomized trial," *AEA Papers and
Proceedings* 110 (2020): 205–209.
5. M. Bertrand, S. E. Black, S. Jensen, and A. Lleras-Muney,
"Breaking the glass ceiling? The effect of board quotas on female
labour market outcomes in Norway," *Review of Economic Studies*
86, no. 1 (2019): 191–239.
6. Agata Maida and Andrea Weber, "Female leadership and gender
gap within firms: Evidence from an Italian board reform," *ILR
Review* (online), October 5, 2020.
7. Joseph Sutherland and Michael G. Miller, "The effect of gender,
party and seniority on interruptions at congressional hearings,"
unpublished working paper, August 20, 2021, https://joesuth.
com/assets/papers/Interruptions_MOC.pdf; .
8. Tonja Jacobi and Dylan Schweers, "Justice, interrupted: The
effect of gender, ideology, and seniority at Supreme Court oral
arguments," *Virginia Law Review* 103 (2017): 1379.
9. Victoria L. Brescoll, "Who takes the floor and why: Gender,
power, and volubility in organizations," *Administrative Science
Quarterly* 56, no. 4 (2011): 622–641.
10. M. J. Lerchenmueller, O. Sorenson, and A. B. Jena, "Gender
differences in how scientists present the importance of their
research: Observational study," *BMJ* 367, no. 8227 (2019): art.
L6573.

11. Christine L. Exley and Judd B. Kessler, "The gender gap in self-promotion," working paper no. 26345, National Bureau of Economic Research, 2019.

12. There is research on gender differences in deception and lying. See Valario Capraro, "Gender differences in lying in sender-receiver games: A meta analysis," *Judgement and Decision Making* 13 (2018): 345–355.

13. Christine L. Exley and Judd B. Kessler, "Why don't women self-promote as much as men?," *Harvard Business Review*, December 2019, https://hbr.org/2019/12/why-dont-women-self-promote-as-much-as-men.

14. Priya Fielding-Singh, Devon Magliozzi, and Swethaa Ballakrishnen, "Why women stay out of the spotlight at work," *Harvard Business Review*, August 2018, https://hbr.org/2018/08/why-women-stay-out-of-the-spotlight-at-work.

15. Tim Bower, "The #MeToo Backlash," *Harvard Business Review*, September–October 2019, https://hbr.org/2019/09/the-metoo-backlash.

16. Shiu-Yik Au, Ming Dong, and Andreanne Tremblay, "How much does workplace sexual harassment hurt firm value?," 2020, available at SSRN, 3437444.

17. Gjergji Cici, Mario Hendriock, Stefan Jaspersen, and Alexander Kempf, "#MeToo meets the mutual fund industry: Productivity effects of sexual harassment," *Finance Research Letters* 40 (2021): art. 101687. The male-dominated mutual fund industry is a particularly appropriate setting for this study given its widespread reputation for sexual harassment, reliance on individual fund managers to make decisions, and fund performance data that are standardized and publicly available.

18. Mark V. Roehling and Jason Huang, "Sexual harassment training effectiveness: An interdisciplinary review and call for research," *Journal of Organizational Behavior* 39, no. 2 (2018): 134–150.

19. Shiu-Yik Au, Andreanne Tremblay, and Leyuan You, "Times up: Does female leadership reduce workplace sexual harassment?," *Academy of Management Proceedings* 2020, no. 1 (2020): art. 21007.

20. Joni Hersch, "Valuing the risk of workplace sexual harassment," *Journal of Risk and Uncertainty* 57, no. 2 (2018): 111–131.

Chapter 5

1. The BRFSS data, while providing information on sexual orientation, are less accurate as income data. Income is reported in categories, and a substantial minority of respondents do not report their incomes.

2. Ariane Hegewisch and Eve Mefford, "The weekly gender wage gap by race and ethnicity: 2020," policy brief #C494, Institute for Women's Policy Research, March 2021, https://iwpr.org/wp-content/uploads/2021/03/2021-Weekly-Wage-Gap-Brief.pdf.

3. In 2018, women were awarded 98,506 advanced degrees, outpacing men substantially in education, health, and biological sciences. Men received 85,568 advanced degrees, dominating in engineering, computer science, and business. As highlighted earlier, women receive only 31.6 percent of doctorates granted in economics. Table 318.30, "Bachelor's, master's, and doctor's degrees conferred by postsecondary institutions, by sex of student and discipline division: 2017–18," Digest of Education Statistics, National Center for Education Statistics, https://nces.ed.gov/programs/digest/d19/tables/dt19_318.30.asp.

4. Ipshita Pal and Jane Waldfogel, "The family gap in pay: New evidence for 1967 to 2013," RSF: The Russell Sage Foundation Journal of the Social Sciences 2, no. 4 (2016): 104–127.

5. Marianne Bertrand, Claudia Goldin, and Lawrence F. Katz, "Dynamics of the gender gap for young professionals in the financial and corporate sectors," American Economic Journal: Applied Economics 2, no. 3 (2010): 228–255.

6. Aline Bütikofer, Sissel Jensen, and Kjell G. Salvanes, "The role of parenthood on the gender gap among top earners," European Economic Review 109 (2018): 103–123.

7. The technique described (and calculated) here is called the Oaxaca-Blinder decomposition. It originated with the nearly simultaneous development by its two namesakes. See Ronald Oaxaca, "Male-female wage differentials in urban labor markets," International Economic Review 14, no. 3 (1973): 693–709 and Alan S. Blinder, "Wage discrimination: Reduced form and structural estimates," Journal of Human Resources 8, no. 4 (1973): 436–455. Detailed explanation of the formula and interpretation can be found in these sources and in most econometrics textbooks.

8. Linda Babcock, Michele Gelfand, Deborah Small, and Heidi Stayn, "Gender differences in the propensity to initiate

negotiations," in *Social Psychology and Economics*, edited by David De Cremer, Marcel Zeelenberg, and J. Keith Murnighan, 239–259 (Mahwah, NJ: Lawrence Erlbaum Associates, 2006).

9. Linda Babcock and Sarah Laschever, *Women Don't Ask* (New York: Bantam Books, 2007).

10. Christine L. Exley, Muriel Niederle, and Lise Vesterlund, "Knowing when to ask: The cost of leaning in," *Journal of Political Economy* 128, no. 3 (2020): 816–854.

11. The results were even worse for Black men, who paid nearly 8 percent more. See Ian Ayres and Peter Siegelman, "Race and gender discrimination in bargaining for a new car," *American Economic Review* 85, no. 3 (1995): 304–321.

12. Katherine Baldiga, "Gender differences in willingness to guess," Management Science 60, no. 2 (2014): 434–448.

13. Katharine Q. Seelye, "Gingrich's 'Piggies' Poked," *New York Times*, January 19, 1995.

14. Andrea Ichino and Enrico Moretti, "Biological gender differences, absenteeism, and the earnings gap," American Economic Journal: *Applied Economics* 1, no. 1 (2009): 183–218.

15. Mariesa A. Herrmann and Jonah E. Rockoff, "Does menstruation explain gender gaps in work absenteeism?," *Journal of Human Resources* 47, no. 2 (2012): 493–508.

Chapter 6

1. Though family caregivers are not expressly listed in Title VII, there are a number of federal statutes that can be used to try to protect them from discrimination in the workplace.

2. Paola Cecchi-Dimeglio, "How gender bias corrupts performance reviews, and what to do about it," *Harvard Business Review*, April 2017.

3. Cody Cook, Rebecca Diamond, Jonathan Hall, John A. List, and Paul Oyer, "The gender earnings gap in the gig economy: Evidence from over a million rideshare drivers," working paper no. 24732, National Bureau of Economic Research, June 2018, http://www.nber.org/papers/w24732.

4. Francine D. Blau and Lawrence M. Kahn, "The gender wage gap: Extent, trends and explanations," *Journal of Economic Literature* 55, no. 3 (2017): 789–865.

5. Benson Rosen and Thomas H. Jerdee, "Influence of sex role stereotypes on personnel decisions," *Journal of Applied Psychology,* 59, no. 1 (1974): 9–14.

6. David Neumark, with assistance from Roy J. Banks and Kyle D. Van Nort, "Sex discrimination in restaurant hiring: An audit study," *Quarterly Journal of Economics* 11, no. 3 (1996): 915–941.

7. Emma Mishel, "Discrimination against queer women in the US workforce: A résumé audit study," *Socius* 2 (2016): art. 2378023115621316.

8. Shelley J. Correll, Stephen Benard, and In Paik, "Getting a job: Is there a motherhood penalty?," *American Journal of Sociology* 112, no. 5 (2007): 1297–1338.

Chapter 7

1. Charles W. Whalen and Barbara Whalen, *The Longest Debate: A Legislative History of the 1964 Civil Rights Act* (Cabin John, MD: Seven Locks Press, 1989), 238.

2. Jo Freeman, "How sex got into title VII: Persistent opportunism as a maker of public policy," *Law and Inequality* 9 (1990): 163.

3. Glass Ceiling Commission, "Glass Ceiling Commission—Good for business: Making full use of the nation's human capital," 1995.

4. David Neumark and Wendy A. Stock, "The labor market effects of sex and race discrimination laws," *Economic Inquiry* 44, no. 3 (2006): 385–419.

5. Jonathan S. Leonard, "Antidiscrimination or reverse discrimination: The impact of changing demographics, Title VII, and affirmative action on productivity," *Journal of Human Resources* 19, no. 2 (1984): 145–174.

6. Elizabeth Hirsh and Youngjoo Cha, "For law and markets: Employment discrimination lawsuits, market performance, and managerial diversity," *American Journal of Sociology* 123, no. 4 (2018): 1117–1160.

7. Fidan Ana Kurtulus, "The impact of affirmative action on the employment of minorities and women: A longitudinal analysis using three decades of EEO-1 filings," *Journal of Policy Analysis and Management* 35, no. 1 (2016): 34–66.

8. Caitlin Knowles Myers, "A cure for discrimination? Affirmative action and the case of California's Proposition 209," *ILR Review* 60, no. 3 (2007): 379–396.

9. Jake Rosenfeld, "Don't ask or tell: Pay secrecy policies in US workplaces," *Social Science Research* 65 (2017): 1–16.

10. Marlene Kim, "Pay secrecy and the gender wage gap in the United States," *Industrial Relations: A Journal of Economy and Society* 54, no. 4 (2015): 648–667.

Chapter 8

1. There are ways that individuals can pay to minimize the risk of poverty that this uncertainty brings. Beyond the scope of the discussion in this chapter, there are annuity products that allow individuals to make a lump sum payment to purchase an annuity that provides a guaranteed monthly payment until death, regardless of how long one lives, and long-term care insurance can help offset extraordinary healthcare costs toward the end of life. The price of these products, then, reflects the insurers' best estimate of future health and mortality patterns among the pool of purchasers.

2. Alicia H. Munnell, "Why the average retirement age is rising," MarketWatch, October 15, 2017, https://www.marketwatch.com/story/why-the-average-retirement-age-is-rising-2017-10-09.

3. The Hispanic paradox has been attributed to the "healthy immigrant" phenomenon: men and women who migrate (to most countries around the world) tend to be healthier than native-born residents of their new countries. See Kyriakos S. Markides and Karl Eschbach, "Aging, migration, and mortality: Current status of research on the Hispanic paradox," *Journals of Gerontology Series B: Psychological Sciences and Social Sciences* 60, special issue 2 (2005): S68–S75.

4. The employee and employer each pay an additional 1.45 percent on all the employee's earnings for Medicare, the health insurance system for elderly individuals.

5. In what follows we refer to a traditional husband-and-wife family, but of course the rules equally apply to same-sex married couples. We also describe scenarios where women earn less than their husbands, but Social Security rules are gender-neutral and a husband is able to collect Social Security based on his wife's (or former wife's) earnings.

6. Social Security Administration, Office of Retirement and Disability Policy, Office of Research, Evaluation, and Statistics, "Fast Facts and Figures About Social Security," publication

no. 13-11785, July 2020, https://www.ssa.gov/policy/docs/cha
rtbooks/fast_facts/2020/fast_facts20.pdf.

7. Privately purchased annuities are available, but these
use actuarial calculations to determine price and payout
combinations. This means that a woman will receive a smaller
monthly benefit than a man at the same purchase price.

8. Slightly more than 10 percent of defined-contribution plans offer
an annuity option that mimics a defined-benefit payout.

9. Vanguard, "How America Saves 2019," Vanguard 2018 Defined
Contribution Plan Data, June 2019, 51, https://pressroom.vangu
ard.com/nonindexed/Research-How-America-Saves-2019-Rep
ort.pdf.

10. 401(k)s do not provide monthly benefits, but the funds can be
available to married partners.

11. Robin L. Lumsdaine and Olivia S. Mitchell, "New developments
in the economic analysis of retirement," *Handbook of Labor
Economics* 3 (1999): 3261–3307.

12. Alicia H. Munnell and Andrew D. Eschtruth, "Modernizing
Social Security: Caregiver credits," issue brief 18-15, Center for
Retirement Research at Boston College, 2018.

13. Matthew S. Rutledge, Alice Zulkarnain, and Sara Ellen King,
"How much does motherhood cost women in Social Security
benefits?," working paper no. 14, Center for Retirement Research
at Boston College, 2017.

FURTHER READING

Averett, Susan L., Laura M. Argys, and Saul D. Hoffman, eds. *Oxford Handbook of Women and the Economy*. New York: Oxford University Press, 2018.

Babcock, Linda, and Sara Lashever. *Women Don't Ask.* New York: Bantam Books, 2007.

Becker, Gary S. *The Economics of Discrimination*. Chicago: University of Chicago Press, 2010. Originally published 1957.

Blau, Francine D., and Lawrence M. Kahn. "The gender wage gap: Extent, trends, and explanations." *Journal of Economic Literature* 55, no. 3 (2017): 789–865.

Canilang, Sara, Cassandra Duchan, Kimberly Kreiss, Jeff Larrimore, Ellen Merry, Erin Troland, and Mike Zabek. "Retirement." *Report of the Economic Wellbeing of US Households in 2019*. Washington, DC: Board of Governors of the Federal Reserve System, 2020. https://www.federalreserve.gov/publications/2020-economic-well-being-of-us-households-in-2019-retirement.htm.

Coontz, Stephanie. *A Strange Stirring: The Feminine Mystique and American Women at the Dawn of the 1960s*. New York: Basic Books, 2011.

Crenshaw, Kimberlé. "Demarginalizing the intersection of race and sex: A black feminist critique of antidiscrimination doctrine, feminist theory and antiracist politics." *University of Chicago Legal Forum* 1989, no. 1 (1989): art. 8.

Goldin, Claudia. "The quiet revolution that transformed women's employment, education, and family." *American Economic Review* 96, no. 2 (2006): 1–21.

Goldin, Claudia, and Lawrence F. Katz, eds. *Women Working Longer: Increased Employment at Older Ages.* Chicago: University of Chicago Press, 2018.

Hersch, Joni, and Jennifer Bennett Shinall. "Fifty years later: The legacy of the Civil Rights Act of 1964." *Journal of Policy Analysis and Management* 34, no. 2 (2015): 424–456.

Heymann, Jody, Bijetri Bose, Willetta Waisath, Amy Raub, and Michael McCormack. "Legislative approaches to nondiscrimination at work: A comparative analysis across 13 groups in 193 countries." *Equality, Diversity and Inclusion: An International Journal* 40, no. 3 (2020): 225–241.

Hoffman, Saul D., and Susan L. Averett. *Women and the Economy: Family, Work and Pay.* New York: Red Globe Press, 2021.

Lundberg, Shelly. "The changing sexual division of labour." In *The Shape of the Division of Labour: Nations, Industries and Households,* edited by Robert M. Solow and Jean-Philippe Touffut. Oxford: Edward Elgar, 2010.

National Committee to Preserve Social Security and Medicare. "Women and retirement: The gender gap persists." Issue brief. n.d. https://www.ncpssm.org/documents/issue-briefs/women-and-retirement-the-gender-gap-persists/.

Neumark, David. "Experimental research on labor market discrimination." *Journal of Economic Perspectives* 56, no. 3 (2018): 799–866.

Sorensen, Elaine. *Comparable Worth: Is It a Worthy Policy?* Princeton, NJ: Princeton University Press, 2019.

INDEX

For the benefit of digital users, indexed terms that span two pages (e.g., 52–53) may, on occasion, appear on only one of those pages.

Tables and figures are indicated by *t* and *f* following the page number